W.G. GRACE ATE MY PEDALO

The Wisden Cricketer
Presents

W.G. GRACE
ATE MY
PEDALO

A Curious Cricket
Compendium

by Tyers & Beach

To subscribe to
The Wisden Cricketer
call 0844 815 0864.

First published in the UK in 2010 by John Wisden & Co
An imprint of A&C Black Publishers Ltd
36 Soho Square, London W1D 3QY
www.wisden.com
www.acblack.com

Reprinted in 2011

ISBN 978 1 4081 3042 1

10 9 8 7 6 5 4 3 2

A CIP catalogue record for this book is available from the British Library.

This book is produced using paper that is made from wood grown in
managed, sustainable forests. It is natural, renewable and recyclable. The
logging and manufacturing processes conform to the environmental
regulations of the country of origin.

Printed and bound by MPG Books in Bodmin, United Kingdom.

CONTENTS

PREFACE

My Great Aunt Bernard, as she was affectionately known to the family, passed away on Christmas Day 2009 and it fell to me to be the executor of her will and effects.

Little did I know that I should unearth perhaps the most significant collection of Victorian cricket periodicals ever held in private hands.

Rummaging through Bernard's fusty old ottoman, I could scarcely contain my excitement at finding these first issues of *The Wisden Cricketer*, whose quarterly 1896 editions are collected in this volume.

Although Great Aunt Bernard lived to a tremendous age, she never married. However, she would occasionally hint at unhappy affairs with some of the great cricketing figures of the late Victorian age, including W.G. himself.

Sadly, these were entirely a figment of Bernard's imagination, as she was quite mad.

I hope very much that these magazines, reprinted exactly as they would have looked in 1896, give you more pleasure than they gave my late great aunt, who grew to hate cricket quite bitterly in her last years, largely as a result of Lalit Modi.

Humphrey Mattingwicket-Lawrence,
Oxford, October 2010

Spring 1896
— The Empire Issue —

THE
WISDEN
CRICKETER

Vol. I - No 1   Spring 1896   Price One Penny

GOD AND GOOGLIES

It is with great pleasure that we present our new periodical, *The Wisden Cricketer*. It is the fervent hope of the publisher that Cricket enthusiasts of all ages will find within its pages a wealth of information, provocative rumination and droll amusement. Should this prove to be lacking, there is a picture of a lady of moderate-to-ill repute in a bathing costume on page 15.

These are most exciting times for the sport of Cricket. Britannia rules the waves, and it is therefore fitting that our first edition should focus on the role of Cricket in the Empire. We are honoured to feature an interview with Dr W.G.

Grace, in which the great batsman offers an explanation for the recent unfortunate matter involving his personage and a pedalo. Also, news of English exploits abroad, some of them cricketing and some military, and some of them a regrettable concoction of the two.

Lastly, we are most extraordinarily fortunate and grateful to have the views of Her Majesty Queen Victoria upon the vexatious question of the fairer sex attempting to play at Cricket.

God Save The Queen, and the sport of Cricket.

—Thos Catchpole, Editor

CORRESPONDENCE
(NO CORRESPONDENCE WILL BE ENTERED INTO)

SIR, I am increasingly certain that there is far too much County Cricket played, of too low a standard, to dwindling crowds. How can our players, and indeed gentlemen, be expected to prepare for the challenge of the Australians when our domestic practice is so inferior?

I advocate a reduction in the number of Counties, perchance even a regional competition, and less emphasis on quantity at the expense of quality. Of course, it will never happen.

Things were better in my day.

—Mjr Theodore Lupus (ret'd),
Cheam

SIR, The decision by MCC to make this summer's Ashes contest available only on pay-per-view daguerreotype is an appallingly short-sighted one that will deprive the younger generation of an opportunity to see their heroes depicted in photographic action. The W.G.s and Ranjis of tomorrow should be able to view Cricket in the more readily available, cheaper lithograph. Or would we lose an entire generation to Association Football and the music hall?

—F.P. Potter,
Newcastle-under-Lyme

SIR, The time has surely come to allow umpires to use all the technology available to them. The 'Moving Pictures' recently developed by those cleverest of Frenchmen, the Brothers Lumières, should be employed to permit reappraisal of contentious decisions. There may be some short break in play - perhaps a week or two - while the 'film' is reviewed, but this is surely a small price to pay for accuracy and fairness?

—D.P. Pennybaker,
Roslyn

W.G. GRACE: MY PEDALO SHAME

England's finest cricketer W.G. held his hand up last night and sensationally admitted: "I WAS inebriated to an unacceptable degree."

The talismanic all-rounder was rapped by Cricket bosses after a late-night carousing session ended in near tragedy following the unlawful piloting of a pedal-propelled pleasure craft.

Doctor Grace, who had been drinking claret all afternoon following England's humiliating defeat to Sudan A, refused to return to quarters at night and instead continued to imbibe in a native watering hole.

VAPOURS

Encouraged by team-mates, Doctor Grace quaffed seven 'Mercury Poisonings', four jugs of 'Matrimonial Relations Upon The Sands' and nine large 'Screaming Feminine Fits Of The Vapours'.

Dis-GRACED

"I've let myself down, I've let Gloucestershire down, I've let the medical profession down, and worst of all, I've let Her Majesty Queen Victoria down," said the contrite sportsman.

> ## "I've let Her Majesty down"

Doctor Grace stole both a native canoe and a bicycle and succeeded in fashioning a primitive pedal-propelled vessel from their component parts.

It is a testament to Doctor Grace's prodigious physical strength that he was able to manoeuvre the ungodly

Fig. 1. The Nautical Velocipede: Doctor Grace Skilfully Navigates His Bastard Craft Through The Straits

hybrid craft 60 miles out into the Red Sea before being caught by the tide.

JOLLY ROGERED

When rescued by the Royal Navy, W.G. was some way out into the Gulf Of Aden and had successfully engaged a small pirate vessel, killing six and teaching the survivors the correct method of hitting to leg.

Doctor Grace initially explained his erratic behaviour as being a result of malaria but subsequently confessed that he had been "disgracefully well-refreshed".

The maritime escapades of their most senior player are merely the latest embarrassment on a tour that has seen England defeated by a variety of native sides, many of whom had to be taught the Laws of Cricket prior to matches.

Lesser Items Of Topical Interest:

MCC HAVE appointed a committee to look into the concerning rise of batsmen's scoring rates. The County Championship last season saw outbreaks of pell-mell batsmanship plunder upwards of one run each over on occasion, prompting concern that the indispensable balance betwixt ball and bat may be under serious threat. Advances in bat-construction technology are thought to be the culprit, along with the introduction of so-called 'training methods'.

THE ZOOTROPE rights for the Eton v Harrow match are to be put to tender on April 3rd, with bids invited from entrepreneurial personages keen to commit to film the contest for later viewing at seaside piers, fairgrounds etc.

THE NEW and exciting *Daily Mail* newspaper, the first edition of which is to be published this May, invites articles, features, comments and curiosities upon the immigrant question, the price of housing and the possibility that travelling gypsies are to set up camp at Lord's Cricket Ground.

A TOURING side, funded by the American industrialist, financier and philanthropist, Sir Allen Roosterbender Stanford III Junior, is to play a series of barnstorming fixtures this summer. Applications are being taken from teams wishing to compete for purses of 20 Guineas, which Sir Allen is personally donating out of the kindness of his heart and with no ulterior motive whatsoever.

ON FEBRUARY 13th at three o'clock, the left-arm bowler and personality P.C.R. Tufnellton will be at Daunt's Bookshop, Mary-le-bone to autograph copies of his most recent publication 'An Hilarious Collection Of Cricketing Mishaps And Anecdotal Tomfooleries'.

THE EDITOR would like to extend warm gratitude to Sir Allen Roosterbender Stanford III Junior for his kind sponsorship of this section.

MRS GATTING'S
NOVELTY MEAT PIES
FOR THE 'ALL-ROUNDER'

SPECIAL PULL-OUT POSTER

THE SENSUAL,
BEGUILING
ALLURE...

...OF THE
ENGLISHMAN
AT BAT.

An Exciting And Accurate Account Of The Match Between Gentlemen of England Versus Players And Natives Of The Cape Colony, February 1896 in Cape Town

After electing to bat, the visitors from the Mother Country were desperately unfortunate to be bowled out for 31 on a brutish pitch.

The natives enjoyed further luck when they came to bat, as the pitch had suddenly and mysteriously become quite excreditable, if fortunate, 895-4.

Some among the English suspected sharp practice or nonspecific rummy goings-on, as the pitch yet again showed its capriciousness, reverting back to its previous wicked deviousness in time for the English second innings (43 all out).

Fig. 1. 'Inspecting The Pitch'

cessively benign, with the result that centuries were scored by fully five of the native order. Naturally, the strokemaking of these uneducated sons of the Veldt was not up to the standard of a County player - the England captain, A.J. 'Rumpy' Nethercote was heard to remark "these poor chaps are scarcely worth a deuce on the off" - but they eventually declared on a

Serendipitously, it was discovered that all five South African centurions have English great-grandparents, and Nethercote had the good sense to telegraph immediately to the Governor of the Cape Colony, who issued them all with certificates confirming that they were born in Hampshire, and thus their runs were credited to the English side.

England XI First Innings

AJ Nethercote *	b Van de Graaf	0
BJ Nethercote	not out	1
SS Flippington-Flop	b Van de Graaf	11
Lord Strokes	c Smuts b Van de Graaf	0
GNER Railway	lbw Botha	6
RPCRQW Bullingdon-Snorter	b Botha	4
GC Cheddar	lbw Botha	1
NWA Compton	c&b Van de Graaf	3
DD Plump †	b Van de Graaf	0
A Coalface	b Botha	0
B Pitpony	b Van de Graaf	0
Extras (lb 3, nb 1, w 1)		5
Total	all out	31

Cape Colony XI First Innings

Johannes Laandegrabbe	b Coalface	87
Piet Pieter *	not out	175
Bakkies Baastaad	lbw Pitpony	191
KK Klop	c Plump b Coalface	160
ODB Smuts †	ret'd out	101
R Krugerrand	not out	103
Extras (b 16, lb 14, nb 12, w 26)		78
Total	for four, declared	895

England XI Second Innings

AJ Nethercote *	b Botha	0
BJ Nethercote	b Van de Graaf	5
SS Flippington-Flop	not out	3
Lord Strokes	c Smuts b Klop	0
GNER Railway	b Botha	0
RPCRQW Bullingdon-Snorter	lbw Krugerrand	11
GC Cheddar	c&b Morkel	12
NWA Compton	b Van de Graaf	7
DD Plump †	c Klop b Smuts	3
A Coalface	c Pieter b Botha	1
B Pitpony	b Baastaad	0
Extras (lb 1)		1
Total	all out	43

Match Awarded to the visitors after five of the home team (Pieter, Baastaad, Klop, Smuts and Krugerrand) were discovered to be English. Umpires: C.J. Nethercote and Miss D.J. Nethercote

Lord West's XI Versus Afrikander XI, Potchefstroom Yachting Club, January 1896

MATCH ABANDONED; BRITISH ARMY SENT FOR

A most unseemly incident marred what had previously been a gentlemanly contest between a strong English XI and a plucky, if untutored, local team.

Resuming after lunch, the English were 18-1 and by no means certain of a commanding total on a troublesome pitch. However, they were indebted to their indomitable opener B.P. 'Kipper' Mantelpiece, who batted most watchfully and correctly.

SUGARY FANCIES

His innings was, perhaps, not one to be savoured by the aesthete; he did not add to his score in the next 38 overs. At a minute before four o'clock, Kipper diligently played out a maiden over, tucked his bat under his arm and began striding off, his thoughts no doubt upon the sugary fancies on offer from the wives of the hosts.

A brouhaha broke out, with the Potchefstroom captain demanding to know where Kipper thought he might be going.

"I always take my tea at four o'clock," said the brave, honest batsman.

The Afrikander spoke quite roughly to Kipper, and intimated that tea in this part of the world was taken at a *quarter past* four o'clock.

Kipper, being a gentleman, naturally acquiesced to the obscene local custom and said nothing. The next over saw a single, and Kipper back on strike.

As the Afrikander left-arm ran in, Kipper quickly whipped out his service revolver and shot himself in the head. As he lay dying, he fixed the Afrikander captain with a firm gaze and told him: "Tea, my boy, is taken at four o'clock."

Fig. 1. 'Kipper Kops It'

Kipper died, but honour was upheld, and the English skipper ensured that justice was done by telegraphing for a regiment of British soldiers, who massacred all the Afrikanders without delay and took possession of the remaining sugary fancies.

LORD WEST'S XI VERSUS AFRIKANDER XI, POTCHEFSTROOM YACHTING CLUB, JANUARY 6 1896

Lord West's XI

Lord West *	b Morkel	0
BP Mantelpiece	retired suicide	3
WO MacTavish	not out	15
Total	for one	18

Match abandoned due to tea-time beastliness, suicidal opener and violent military struggle.

LETTER FROM ABROAD

FROM OUR OWN CORRESPONDENT: GENERAL KITCHENER, KHARTOUM

It is vilely hot here, and one cannot get a decent houseboy for love nor money. For amusement, we have taught the locals Cricket, and several of the brutes have shown no little aptitude. The Sudanese physique is well-suited for quick bowling, and two fellows in particular have given some of our batsmen no end of difficulty in the nets.

However, it was discovered that they had been tampering with the ball - there being no other explanation for the success they were enjoying against some of our officers - and I had no choice but to have them both shot as a warning to others.

Happily, the native bowlers have been unable to get the ball to deviate off the straight and narrow since, and order has been restored. I myself scored an especially correct century yesterday afternoon, leaving the native tweakers positively despondent as a result, especially the adult males.

Thus we win the battle for hearts and minds.

God Save The Queen.

Being An Illuminating Intercourse With His Excellency Bahadur Jadeja Choudhurani, Nawab of Dhaka

Readers will be excited by a rare treat this issue: a most welcome opportunity to learn more about the Indian batting marvel His Excellency Bahadur Jadeja Choudhurani, Nawab of Dhaka - known to all as 'Keith'.

The last County season was illuminated by the masterful strokeplay of His Excellency for Cambridge University, Sussex and Combined Aristocrats. One and all have marvelled at his exquisite timing through cover, his precise leg-play and his surprising proficiency as a public house brawler.

In 1895, Keith achieved the prestigious double of scoring 2,000 runs and being spoken to by police five times before the end of June. Does he have any words of advice for our younger readers?

"The most crucial matter is to be always spotting the length of the delivery early," he says. "And then giving the fucker a bloody good whack. Honestly, the way people bang on about batting, you'd think it was a fucking ballet or something. See it, hit it, get off the park and have a bloody good drink."

POINT, AND INDEED,
COUNTER-POINT:

SHOULD LADIES BE ENCOURAGED TO PLAY CRICKET?

PROPOSING:
WILLIAM GLADSTONE,
THE PRIME MINISTER

Indisputably they should. There are few sights more splendid than a young Englishwoman haring in off her long-run or hoisting up her petticoats to caress one through the covers. Naturally, there is a question of propriety with regard to revealing the lower half of the female form, but this might be overcome by having the lady players attired like young boys. What could be more wholesome and right than a languid summer afternoon spent watching an assemblage of the better sort of young English woman, dressed as a boy, full of spunk, and attempting to undo one another with a devilish tweak?

RENOUNCING:
HER MAJESTY
QUEEN VICTORIA

We are not amused, not even in the slightest part, by the suggestion. A woman has no more place upon a cricket field than her husband would in a kitchen or a hospital at the time of childbirth. The mere idea is preposterous to the point of grotesquery and, if we may speak entirely frankly, we doubt that it is even a serious proposition. Surely no female would attempt to play at Cricket when there are so many pastimes more suitable to our sex, including wearing an enormous hat made of diamonds, giving birth, baiting the Irish and unlicensed boxing.

THE WISDEN CRICKETER
IMAGINES...WHAT MIGHT
A LADY CRICKETER
LOOK LIKE?

Fig 1. Our young gamine embraces a close friend at start of play.

Fig 2. By the end of the innings physical exertion has hardened her features to those of a Man-Lady.

THE WONDERFUL & MYSTERIOUS WORLD WHICH SURROUNDS US

FACIODEDUCTIOLOGY

THE LATEST SCIENTIFIC CRAZE AND HOW CRICKET IS IN THE VANGUARD OF ITS APPLICATION

It has long been established that much can be learned about the character of a man by the simple study of his facial features. The Spanish shopkeeper, with his dark complexion and sensuous, lidded eyes, is prone to lasciviousness and needing to sleep in the afternoons; the canny Scot, distinguished by his thin, sallow features, likes nothing better than a careful auditing of his personal finances or a nip of whisky; and the honest and cheerful English tradesman's ruddy, open face references a humble and hardworking character, provided he is spoken to firmly and directly.

But the march of progress is ever swift, and what had previously been mere intuition has become crystallised in a new and exacting science: *Faciodeductiology*. The infant discipline's most celebrated practitioner is the impressive Dr Aubrey Fotheringhay, the brilliant physician who was until recently resident in Harley Street.

Dr Fotheringhay
MD MDMA GBH

Happily, notably for readers of this journal, Cricket finds itself at the forefront of this new science. Dr Fotheringhay, himself a recreational batsman of no little ability, has focused his attentions upon some of the country's leading cricketers. Here, he takes up the story.

"Cricketers are inexpensive, easily procured and tend towards moral feebleness, meaning they can be easily lured into a laboratory for diagnosis," says the scientist.

Dr Fotheringhay's virile young assistant, Fabrice, procures a Minor Counties Player outwith an East End Gin Palace

"My first subject was Mr I.R. Bell of Warwickshire. He was referred to me by his family doctor, who had become baffled by Bell's persistent failure to convert a promising start into a significant score. His general practitioner wondered if I could deduce anything about Bell's character and batsmanship from his visage.

"I conducted a series of experiments on the batsman's face, precisely measuring the size and distribution of his features with sophisticated devices, and applying various chemical concoctions to his skin, partly for the purposes of research but predominately for my own amusement. I concluded that his eyes were perhaps a tiny fraction wider apart than the average man's, and that this suggested a total dearth of moral fibre and a tendency to play around the front pad."

Dr Fotheringhay kept Bell in

STUDIES IN FACIODEDUCTIOLOGY

*Dr Fortheringhay wishes to thank Prof. K.T. Gimp of the Lucerne Institute
For Applied Pogonolgy for first sight of his recent paper
'The Aero-Dynamical possibilities of the Handlebar Moustache'*

(A) NASAL-GAZING — EVALUATING PROBOSCIPAL PROTUBERANCE FOR
INDICATIONS OF MORAL WEAKNESS AND POOR SLIP CATCHING

Short Stop   *Long Hop*   *In The Air*   *Up and Over*   *Howzat*

(B) CRYPTO-NAPERY — DETERMINING A FIELDER'S BEST POSITION
BY STARING AT THE BACK OF HIS HEAD

Long On   *Mid Off*   *Long Off*   *Extra Cover*

Mid Wicket   *Deep Mid Wicket*   *Silly Point*

his laboratory for some weeks, but the nimble right-hander managed to escape through a window and was cowardly enough to make his case to the authorities. Subsequently, Dr Fotheringhay found himself the subject of unwelcome attention from the police and had to leave his Harley Street practice for a more modest, but secluded, coal cellar in Hackney Marsh.

From there he has begun his greatest feat yet: proving that the young Essex opener Mr A.N. Cook is a maniac bent upon the violent destruction of the entire human race, as evidenced by the pedestrian left-hander's unusually luxuriant eyebrows.

(c) PROTOPRANDIAL PROFILING — EXAMINING THE RELATIONSHIP BETWEEN EYEBROW ANGLING AND A PROPENSITY FOR PLAYING ON

Full Yorker

Across The Line

Leg Cutter

(d) ADVANCED JOWLERY — DETECTING A BOWLER'S ACTION FROM THE VOLUPTUOUSNESS OR OTHERWISE OF HIS JAWLINE

Slow Left Arm

Wristy Tweaker

Swings Both Ways

Fast-Medium

Military Medium

Foreign

Dr Fotheringhay has written repeated communications to the government, the police and Mr G.A. Gooch of Essex County Cricket Club yet, at the time of writing, Cook remains at large, despite the best efforts of Dr Fotheringhay to catch him at Chelmsford in a large butterfly net.

THE ABSTRACT AND BRIEF CHRONICLES OF THE TIME

THIS MONTH, AN EXAMINATION OF THE PLIGHT OF THE TOURING CRICKET PROFESSIONAL

"When wus went on the expedition wi' Lord Rosebery to Tasmania, wor youngest, Tommy, was nobbut a tiny bairn. By the time wus'd come back on the steamship, the lad was already opening the burling for Ashington and he had a beard that made Dr Grace look like Marie Lloyd"
—S.J. HARMISON OF NORTHERN COUNTIES AND ENGLAND.

This is but one heart-wrenching anecdote from a cricketer endeavouring to be both a father and a fast bowler for England.

To the untutored reader, what could be more wonderful than travelling around the globe, playing Cricket, seeing the world with the fellows, and all under the glorious flag of Britannia? Surely these chaps have won first prize in the lottery of life!

GRUELLING

Yet the reality is often very different. In the case of the professional bowler quoted above, he was obliged to travel to Tasmania on a steamship and play a gruelling series of matches against local teams. Gentler readers should be advised that the next piece of information is distressing: he was often expected to play as many as two games in three months.

So long did the passage back to England take, he says, his children had grown in his absence and he returned to find the village he called home had totally disappeared. Even his own wife did not recognise him, nor he her. Presuming him dead, she had married again, to a local policeman who threw Harmison in the cells.

"My entire life was ruined by the sport of Cricket," says Harmison. "And I'm not the only one. One lad I know was sent for as a replacement on Lord Russell's tour of Rhodesia. All the bowlers they took with them were eaten by hippopotamuses, and so they telegraphed for more.

Fig. 1. A typical native pitch

"By the time he got there from Manchester, the entire touring party was dead of old age and he had to face a useful native side all on his own, and they were furious at having to wait 15 years to complete their innings so they went and ate him on the spot."

Fig. 2. The local dish of 'Curry'

GRILLING

Even for the cricketer who survives cannibalistic natives who refuse to go off for bad light, or does not find his entire family ripped from his bosom by the jackbooted constabulary, there are further pitfalls to the playing of Cricket outside these shores.

"It is hot, and the food can be terrible," said Harmison. "If I had one piece of advice for young cricketers, it would be to avoid foreign places like you would consumption or people from Sunderland."

Ask Uncle Cricket!

A TOPIC OF THE UTMOST SERIOUSNESS

Gather round, young fellows. Uncle Cricket must speak to you about a grave matter.

Spring is upon us! Kindly old Sol starts to show his face, the birds sing, the very air seems to scent of hope and promise. The country lad can look out of his window and see the lamb gambolling, and the horny-handed, loyal rustic type butchering the creature for the Easter table of the well-to-do. Both the rustic old man and the lamb know that this is their place in the order of things.

Meanwhile in the cities, the young 'townie' can gaze out of *his* window and see the splendidly-dressed ladies and gentlemen going about their business, perhaps to a light opera or a stimulating exhibit. And perchance one of the gentlemen will be occasioned to thrash an uppity beggar or street-tough for using coarse language in the presence of his lady companion, possibly aided in the dispensation of this justice by a passing policeman or three. This too is the right and correct way of the universe.

And so in life, so on the cricket field: order, justice and the right spirit. Which is why the recent shocking spate of dissent, petulance and querying of the umpire's decision must be quashed without delay or debate. The sight of an England bowler shaking his head in disagreement with an LBW verdict, or raising an eyebrow at a not-out decision, is beyond any doubt the most disgusting spectacle in modern English life today, with the possible exception of the Labour movement. It is wrong, it is cowardly, it is wicked; and it may yet lead to the total collapse of Her Majesty's Empire.

Let Uncle Cricket be perfectly clear: it is to stop. With Spring upon us, some of you young chaps are no doubt feeling quite lusty and excitable. Put aside your thoughts of 'showing off' to your fellows, or querying the word of your elders and betters. Not all boys have a papa who is on the noble game's disciplinary committee, and they should do well to remember it.

FOR THE LADY

EDITED BY OUR FEMININE
ISSUES CORRESPONDENT,
MR WILLIAM BABCOCK

THE EXCITING
OPPORTUNITIES AVAILABLE
TO LADIES REGARDING THE
SPORT OF CRICKET

It has long been held that the fairer s-x has no place at Cricket beyond spectating (in silence, and without troubling her husband with vexatious questions).

But social change is upon us, not just in commerce, science and military conquest, but in matters that females can understand also. Perhaps within a hundred years, ladies will not only be watching Cricket regularly, but grasping some of its simpler Laws, or even winning the frequent praise of their men by assisting in the preparation of tea-time provisions.

Naturally, this ambition must be weighed against the preposterous claims of self-styled 'womanists' who argue that a lady could actually *play* Cricket! There is a word for such a female, and it is not a nice word, I am afraid to say. That word is 'harlot'.

NOTICE OF AN EVENT

The next in Mrs Edith Ladygarden's lecture series 'Correct Procedures For The Dismissal Of Household Staff' will be delivered at the Wigmore Hall on February 8th at 7 o'clock. The topic will be 'How to remove an obdurate scullery maid with a jagging leg-cutter'. Tea, cakes and laudanum will be sold.

RECOMMENDED:
*Dr Humbert Postlethwaite's
Patented Feminine Talcum Powder:
Extraordinarily Efficacious in the
Treatment of a Sticky Wicket.*

DR GRACE'S SCHOOL FOR CRICKET

LESSON ONE: CORRECT DEFENSIVE POSTURE WHEN FACED WITH HOSTILE NATIVE BOWLING

THE GENTLEMAN'S GUARD
*Right knee raised; cheroot
angled to Leg.*

THE NOBLESSE OBLIGE
Dressed to Leg; pocket-watch to Off.

THE BARONET'S BLOCK
Moustache advisable.

**THE CODPIECE
COMME IL FAUT**
Middle stump guard.

THE VISCOUNT'S REVERSE
Hat optional.

THE PALMERSTON SNOOZE
A Runner may be required.

THE WISDEN CRICKETER IS PROUD TO PRESENT
A STORY IN FOUR PARTS BY MR AUGUSTUS CLOOT, WHO
WAS RECENTLY AWARDED THE SOCIETY OF AUTHORS'
PRESTIGIOUS 'MOST DISTURBED NOVELIST' MEDAL
(SPORTING FICTION SECTION).

THE PAVILION OF HORRORS

Oh! How hard the work was!

Eliza Tanner, 18 years old, slight and on the short side, put down the scrubbing brush and sighed. Sweeping a stray lock of auburn hair away from her pretty, rather bold face, she surveyed the huge expanse of floor in the Long Room. It was her lot to scrub this noble chamber every morning, and with a brush no bigger than the palm of her small, calloused hand. A portrait of W.G. stared down fiercely at her, as if demanding to know why she had stopped.

Eliza measured the room with a weary eye. She had polished from the walnut cabinet containing the talismanic undergarments of Lumpy Stevens to the embalmed dray horse fatally struck by a Fuller Pilch drive up at Sheffield, yet it was barely a sixth portion of the whole. Mrs Mordeth would be around directly and there would be hell to pay if the floor wasn't shining like the pate of the talkative Leicestershire wicketkeeper P.A. Nixon, and Eliza, with 13 younger siblings and her dipsomaniac parents to support back in Whitechapel, was desperately needful of the employment.

Even so, she might have found a position nearer home, but Eliza had a secret passion: cricket. It remained unspoken for fear of ridicule (or worse, dismissal) but, although her work at Lord's was hard and lowly, she could spend a few hours each day covertly watching some of the matches at the great ground, or - better yet - observe the MCC players in the nets.

The dashing left-hander J.T. 'Johnny' Brawnston-Smyth was her favourite: the precise foot movement to the short delivery, the sure judgement of length, the commanding range of shots through the off-side. She blushed a little as she admitted to herself that his fine frame and strong, proud features did no harm. Would that she could speak to him one day!

S he put down the brush as she allowed herself to day-dream that she was sat outside the Pavilion, clad in as fine a frock as any lady in London, watching Johnny score a forceful century against the Australians. And then he would walk off, undefeated on 136, his fair hair flapping in the wind as he raised his bat to acknowledge the applause, before his eyes locked on Eliza's and he swept her up in his arms, those arms powerful yet supple from delicate strokes through cov—

"Eliza Tanner! What are you a-bleedin' sittin' there starin' for, gal?"

Mrs Mordeth was standing over her, a large woman with the powerful shoulders of an Afrikander quick bowler - and the temper, too. She grabbed Eliza by the ear and pulled it, hard.

"To think that I was so kind as to give employment to a common, lazy slattern such as you. I'm too tender-hearted, that's my problem, everyone says so."

"Sorry ma'am, yes ma'am."

"Oh you will be, my gal. Meantimes, you are to run to the Nursery Ground and attend to a lady. One of the gentlemen's fiancées is here to visit, but himself is still practising at the nets. You're to show her where she can wait in comfort."

"Yes ma'am," said Eliza. "Which of the gentlemen is she betrothed to?"

"Not that it's any business of yours, you nosy trollop, but she's to be married to Mr Brawnston-Smyth at the end of this County season."

Eliza gasped in shock and sadness.

"No!"

Mrs Mordeth regarded her with a sly, appraising eye.

"Sweet on him, are you?" she sneered, and Eliza's heart sank at the accuracy of the woman's line and length. "As if a fine batsman such as that would even look at a little sewer rat like you."

She cackled, and gave Eliza's ear one last tweak, this time in the opposite direction, like Bosanquet fiddling out a groping tailender.

Eliza scuttled away before the brute could see her tears. Mrs Mordeth was right: how stupid to dream that someone like Mr Brawnston-Smyth could ever take interest in a scullery girl. Eliza ran.

Still upset, she found herself presently at the Nursery Ground - but could see no lady waiting there. Bemused, Eliza made for the groundsman's hut. Perhaps old Mr Hunt had seen this lady. Even if not, Eliza might glean some interesting titbit about pitch preparation, or whether he thought it would swing tomorrow morning for the visit of mighty Yorkshire. She hurried across the turf and was about to knock on the door when a ghastly, blood-curdling scream came from within.

"Mr Hunt!" shouted Eliza. "Are you hurt?"

She rattled at the door, but it was locked. A groan came from inside. Eliza tugged with all her might at the handle, but it would not come. Suddenly, the door was flung open, knocking Eliza backwards onto the turf. She could see Mr Hunt, slumped in the corner, blood pouring from a wound in the side of his neck. And in the doorway, a very tall, severely beautiful, pale lady in a long gown.

Eliza gasped as she looked up at her. A trail of dark blood dripped from the side of the woman's full lower lip. Slowly, and quite without compunction, a long, lascivious tongue lashed out to lick it back into her wide red mouth.

"My name is Honoraria Wellington. I expect you are here to take me to my Johnny?"

Eliza eventually managed to stammer: "B-b-but... Mr Hunt. What have you done to him? Is he alright?"

"Oh him?" laughed Miss Wellington, a laugh crisp and icy, a laugh to freeze even the June warmth of the Nursery Ground. "He is quite fine. I feed on him occasionally, which he adores. Don't you, creature?"

Mr Hunt was now slumped back, a dreamy look on his face, as if in another world.

"You are... a vampire?" gasped Eliza.

Miss Wellington gazed hard into Eliza's eyes, and it felt as if she were looking deep into her very soul.

"What is your name, child?" she asked. She reached out to stroke Eliza's cheek with a soft, exquisitely cold hand. Eliza's breath came faster: she felt at once very afraid of Miss Wellington and yet also in her thrall, like an English batsman facing the Demon Spofforth.

"Eliza, if it please you, ma'am."

"What a pretty girl you are,

Eliza," murmured Miss Wellington. "I am sure I shall like you very much. You seem the sort of girl who knows when to keep her mouth shut."

"Oh yes, ma'am," said the terrified Eliza. "I am. I really am. I promise."

"Well, that is splendid," said Miss Wellington. "I am sure we will be the best of friends."

The hand stopped stroking Eliza's hot cheek.

"Because if you speak even one word of this" - the hand was gripping Eliza's cheek now, hard, pinching her face - "Then I shall cut out your heart and eat it here on the Nursery Ground during the tea interval."

Eliza nodded, dumbstruck.

Miss Wellington released her.

"What a super day for cricket," she said. "Now let us go and find my Johnny."

To Be Continued...

WHAT NEXT FOR BRAVE ELIZA? IS THE DASHING MCC BATSMAN ALSO A GHOULISH IMBIBER OF BODILY FLUIDS? OR IS JOHNNY INCOGNISANT OF HIS INTENDED'S HIDEOUS CONDITION? AND WILL GROUNDSMAN HUNT BE ABLE TO PREPARE A SPORTING DECK FOR THE VISIT OF YORKSHIRE, MAULED AS HE HAS BEEN BY A MEMBER OF THE UNDEAD COMMUNITY?
FIND OUT IN THE NEXT THRILLING INSTALMENT OF
THE PAVILION OF HORRORS...

ALSO IN THE FORTHCOMING ISSUE!

An interview with the polymath C.B. Fry – on maths... An investigation into the links between Freemasonry and Umpiring... Cricket and the Chinese Question – Packing the leg-side as a deterrent?... A colourful poster of the splendid Indian batsman, Ranji, shooting what appears to be a tiger or possibly an armoire... Cocaine and the modern cricketer...

INSTRUCT YOUR MAN TO PROCURE A COPY POSTHASTE!

BOOK REVIEWS BY OUR
LITERARY CORRESPONDENT,
MONTGOMERY 'INKY'
PATTERSON

DAS KAPITAL

BY KARL MARX

This is a superb book by one of the finest cricket writers currently wielding the pen. Herr Marx offers brilliant insight into the trials of the 'leftie' in the modern world: from the difficulties of bowling into footmarks while maintaining control of the ball, to the setting of fields when delivering medium-pace from around the wicket, there is scarce anything in the cack-hander's repertoire that is not ably covered. Were I able to read German, I am sure I should enjoy it even more. Bravo, Herr Marx!

BLACK BEAUTY

BY A GHASTLY DO-GOODING FEMALE WHOSE NAME ESCAPES ME

H.P. Hutchinson of Leicestershire

This book is devoted entirely to the adventures of a horse, but is sadly without any merit whatsoever. Incredibly, it makes no mention of the Leicestershire seam bowler H.P. 'Horseface' Hutchinson, nor does it touch upon the exploits of that much-loved denizen of The Oval, P.D.Q. Wode, who once scored a century before lunch for Surrey and then ran all the way to Epsom to ride Merry Frederick to victory in the Derby.

When I inform you that it even omits to discuss the famous incident where Lord Hawke punched the 1887 Grand National winner, Old Jack, in the eye after the animal moved behind the bowler's arm at Scarborough, I am sure you will agree that the 'lady writer' of this book is little short of a disgrace.

MRS CECILY BEASTING
ANSWERS YOUR
CORRESPONDENCE IN
MATTERS OF ETIQUETTE,
DECORUM AND KEEPING
A STRAIGHT BAT. THIS
MONTH, A SELECTION OF
YOUR ENQUIRIES IN REGARD
TO THE OFTEN THORNY
ISSUE OF FOREIGNERS

Dear Mrs Beasting,

Help me, Mrs Beasting: you are my only hope. My youngest sister, a kind-hearted but foolish girl, recently undertook missionary work in Australia. She is rather high-minded and travelled there full of insistences that they could be taught how to practise Christianity, behave properly while spectating at Cricket, enter the pavilion correctly attired and such. Naturally, we were extremely concerned. But now communication reaches us that she has 'fallen for' and wishes to marry an Australian - and a bowler, at that. What on earth are we to do?

—*Flora Whittington,*
Barnes Village

My Dear Miss Whittington,

Firstly, I must offer my sincerest condolences. No respectable family ought to suffer such a hurtful indignity. Would that your sister had died of dysentery on the voyage over. The correct course of action is to pretend, in fact, that this is exactly what has happened, and hope that the Australian murders her in a fit of drunken rage, as he is surely likely to do.

—*Mrs Cecily Beasting*

Dear Mrs Beasting,

My club has invited an Afrikander to come and lodge with us during the next English summer and play some Cricket. Naturally, we all wish to make the fellow welcome, but are unsure as to how he will fit in. Have you any experience in such matters?

—*B. Bainbridge,*
Cannock

Sir,

The Afrikander is relatively straightforward to care for and requires no more than a bed of straw, three meals of raw meat (horse, badger, urchin, etc) per diem and the occasional pint of beer. They can make quite acceptable companions and batsmen.

Under no circumstances encourage the Afrikander to mate with a local girl: they have been known to escape and displace local wildlife, which they can outbreed with astonishing efficiency, with potentially devastating implications for the purity of Cricket within our borders.

—Mrs Cecily Beasting

 # PERSONAL NOTICES

TINY Australian hooking monkey seeks other for companionship, breeding and possibly more. Enquiries to Ponting's Animal Curiosities, Hobart, Tazmania.

FOR sale: Prince Albert Signature Abdominal Protector, one careful owner. Apply Buckingham Palace.

WANTED for import to England: South Africans who can and will play cricket. Apply at Lord's.

WILLIAM. I am sorry for ridiculing your Short Leg. Forgive me? Wilhelmina

---

WORKING Men of England! There are opportunities for advancement in the colonies for wicketkeepers, tail-end batsmen and left-arm fast men. Apply to: James Lilywhite, The Haymarket.

NOTICE From The Bishop Of York: It has been brought to the attention of the Vicar of St Stephen's, Skipton that a Local Woman has been encouraging working men of the environ to sneak away from their toil and play Cricket in the rectory garden. This must be stopped forthwith; the authorities have been notified.

ASPIRING young cricketer, gentle, lyrical, fond of Wilde and wristyleg play, aches to meet same. Meet at Magdalene College Cambridge, by punting jetty, Thursdays.

CURIOUS as to the black magick of ball-tampering, seam-picking and other sinister tomfoolery? Have you considered the potentials of teeth? Learn more in this useful handbook, delivered to you in discreet, plain-brown wrapping paper. Send monies to Mr S. Afridi, The Old Dentistry, Barking.

BATSMAN wants beard. PO Box 224, London.

FACTS ABOUT W.G. GRACE

Doctor Grace has only ever vomited once: it was into a large tureen of parsnip soup, shortly after being presented to the Bishop of Galway and Kilmacduagh.

Doctor Grace consumes a Double Gloucester cheese every second day, irregardless of whether he is hungry or not.

Doctor Grace's name if he were a Frenchman would be *Docteur Grâce*, and he would eat nothing but Roquefort.

Doctor Grace once indecently assaulted Otto von Bismarck, the Chancellor of Germany.

Doctor Grace once mistook a street urchin for a chair and crushed the boy quite badly. Luckily, Doctor Grace was not hurt.

Doctor Grace is a dedicated supporter of the writings of Mr Charles Darwin, and believes that the Australian may one day 'evolve' into a passable human being.

Doctor Grace can run faster than any man alive, provided the race takes place in the Doctor's private gymnasium.

Doctor Grace was decorated for heroism for his part in the Battle of Kandahar (1890), although he remained in Gloucestershire throughout the campaign as he has an aversion to the heat.

A 24-HOUR PERIOD IN THE DAILY EXISTENCE OF...

THE REVEREND M.L. HAYDEN

OPENING BATSMAN, MUSCULAR CHRISTIAN, COOK

FIVE O'CLOCK...

I am up to salute the new day, a day of awesomeness, competitiveness and applying myself to the greater glory of God and the Baggy Green. I start with an excursion into the sea on my wooden surfing board. The sea is almost entirely flat, like a billiard table; there are some small children paddling. I sledge them for several minutes, for their own good.

SIX O'CLOCK...

Early to Matins, where I give a most enthusiastic sermon about my recent 'surf', stressing how incredibly tough the conditions were and how I had to work most diligently for my reward.

EIGHT O'CLOCK...

Return to the beach, where the children are still crying. If they cannot toughen up, they will never succeed in the competitive hothouse that is international paddling. I offer them a beer and a handshake but they decline. Perhaps they are English. They certainly whine enough.

NINE O'CLOCK...

Go into the Bush with my close friend the Reverend Symonds, where we spend the day wrestling naked and stabbing animals.

A QUARTER PAST SIX...

Return home, practise staring into the mirror and chewing in an aggressive manner.

EIGHT O'CLOCK...

Fashion a simple repast of my own recipe: kangaroo profiteroles on a bed of leaves and wallaby's colon. Retire for the night.

TEN O'CLOCK...

Pray to God for a bit, but this degenerates into a sledging contest with The Almighty, who I fear may be a Pommie after all, the way He cometh the raw prawn with me. Sleep.

Maharajah L. Modi of Jaipur & The East India Company
In Partnership With Moores' Famous Mercury Throat Lozenges
('A Most Riveting Tingling Sensation') Present:

A 'TWENTY AND TWENTY' CRICKETING TOURNAMENT TO BE KNOWN AS THE:

INDIAN TERRITORIES PRE-EMINENT LEAGUE

IN REGARDS to the not inconsiderable augmentation of interest in the sport of Cricket amongst the Natives of the Indian colonies, it has been agreed that a tournament be sanctioned allowing some of the Indians to form their own teams.

TO EDUCATE the Natives in the correct manner of playing the game, a number of the most exalted English players of the present day will participate, including Mr 'Fat' Freddie Flintstone, the dipsomaniac demon bowler of Preston and reputed thirstiest man in The North.

ALSO JOINING Mr F.F. Flintstone (sobriety permitting) will be the amazing cricketing Irishman Mr E.I.E.I.O. Morgan and P. Collingwood, the noted North country stonewaller credited with inventing the exciting 'nurdle to leg' stroke.

IT IS anticipated that aspiring cricketers from the colonies will gain inestimable insight into the game from watching these English titans.

THE TOURNAMENT organisers are most keen to stress that no player shall forgo any Cricket for his country or county side as a result of commitments to the Indian Pre-Eminent League.

ALL CAN AND SHOULD FOLLOW THE EXCITING NEW SPECTACLE!

36

Summer 1896
— Family & Society —

THE
WISDEN
CRICKETER

VOL. I - No 2   SUMMER 1896   PRICE ONE PENNY

From the New Editor

In this publication's first issue, we ruminated upon the role of Cricket in Empire. In this, our Family & Society edition, we turn to the part the game has to play at Home.

Our great country faces considerable challenges as the new century approaches: the declining health of our beloved Queen, the gap between rich and poor and the proposed changes to the LBW law to name but three. But let us not send in the nightwatchman of fear, but rather pad up the dashing middle-order of heart, courage and mindless optimism.

From the slums of Manchester, where philanthropists from MCC are distributing bats and pads among the poor, to the desperate depravity of Whitechapel, where the wives of County members are entreating prostitutes to turn their backs on wickedness and learn to prepare teas for cricketers, our game has its part to play in shaping the country.

On a personal note, if I may, might I say what an honour it is to be appointed editor of this young magazine, albeit in trying circumstances. That my predecessor should have been killed by falling masonry while briefly resting his eyes in a gutter after a hard day's work is a tragedy for Cricket, for journalism and perhaps most of all for the public houses of the Fleet Street area. I shall shoulder his burden as best I can.

—Bartholomew Shipman,
Editor-At-Large

40

CORRESPONDENCE
(NO CORRESPONDENCE WILL BE ENTERED INTO)

SIR, All of us must make sacrifices in his profession or employment. Why should England cricketers be different? The recent spate of England men missing Test matches simply to attend to a sick child is frankly a dereliction of duty. Would some of the titans of old have passed up the chance of a crack at the Aussies just to go and blub at their first-born's bedside just because it had typhoid or whooping cough? Of course not.

−*G.K. Snodgrass,*
Epping Forest

SIR, I recently purchased a copy of Mr Periwig's estimable 'Boys I Have Beaten' and I am bound to say that it made quite an impression upon me. If a few more players of today were to feel Mr Periwig's switch around their posteriors, I am quite certain that the England XI might not be in such a parlous state.

−*Mrs O.G. Beater-Keate,*
Windsor

SIR, This crop of fast bowlers from the North East of England is all well and good, but we must not lose sight of the broader picture. While this battery of lanky 'Geordie' fastmen is off playing at Cricket, who is mining the coal? I am no industrial expert, but I cannot believe that the Empire can grow as powerful on useful three-wicket hauls and heartbreaking tales of homesickness as it can on coal and steel. I am sorry to say that these men are little better than traitors.

−*A.K.A. Potteringay,*
Derby

CRICKETING IRISHMAN DISCOVERED

GOOD-NATURED CURIOSITY HAS EXCEPTIONAL RANGE OF SCORING SHOTS AND SURPRISING COMMAND OF ENGLISH LANGUAGE

BY OUR IRISH ISSUES CORRESPONDENT, MR HENRY SPODE IN MAYFAIR

After Dr Livingstone's shocking discovery of The Frenchman Who Washed His Hands and the Amazing Charitable Scotsman unearthed by Sir Henry Morton Stanley on the Isle Of Bute last summer, a third sensational finding has been made: that of an Irish Batsman.

The individual, one E.I.E.I.O. Morgan, was spotted in his native country by the adventurer, botanist and Cricket enthusiast Dr Henry Rutherford.

"A batsman of rare talent"

Dr Rutherford successfully tethered Morgan and imported him to London, where he was immediately co-opted into MCC and given a debut for England against Indian Territories at The Oval, scoring 134 in just an hour and a half.

The good doctor has for some years concentrated his endeavours on tracking and capturing cricketers in the Cape Colonies, but recently decided to search for potential England players closer to home.

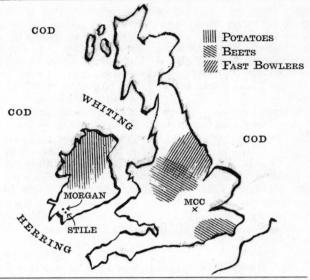

COD

POTATOES
BEETS
FAST BOWLERS

COD

WHITING

COD

MORGAN

MCC
×

STILE

HERRING

Fig. 1. Ireland. Left at Wales and up a bit.

"I had long suspected that cricketers might be found in Ireland," says Dr Rutherford. "The wet weather, and the populace's fondness for starch-based food-stuffs, alcoholic capacity and innate desire for hitting things seemed to me ideal soil from which to harvest cricketers.

SNAKES

"I approached MCC about potential funding or sponsorship for my expedition, but they were, to speak frankly, quite dismissive.

"The chairman of the MCC Foreigner Procurement Com-mittee told me categorically that there were absolutely no cricketers whatsoever in Ireland, because they had been driven out, along with the snakes, by Saint Patrick. MCC would not give me a penny."

Dr Rutherford vowed to prove the doubters wrong. He raised the necessary money for his expedition by manufacturing and selling low-grade opiates to the poor of Whitechapel and the worst bits of Manchester, and sailed to Ireland in March to begin his search.

"Six weeks passed and I had found nothing of any note," he

says. "The closest I had come was in Limerick, when one of my assistants caught sight of what initially appeared to be a wicketkeeper, but turned out to be an unusually shaped stile. I confess that I began to lose heart."

At his darkest hour, however, Mother Cricket smiled upon Dr Rutherford.

TREE

"I was some short distance South of Dublin when I came upon Morgan sitting under a tree. So exasperated was I by the apparent futility of my search, I offered the fellow a few small silver coins if he would pick up a bat and attempt to play a few shots. It was a quite desperate move on my behalf, I freely admit - but what extraordinary results it yielded!"

The untutored Celt was soon smiting balls this way and that, even inventing entirely new shots in the process and angling the doctor's deliveries to all parts of the ground (i.e. paddock).

"I knew immediately that I had found a batsman of rare talent, so I hit him over the head and shipped him back to England," says the doctor.

Within days Morgan had been signed by Middlesex, and was soon declared a British Subject by special intervention of the Home Secretary. His contributions to the England team seem certain to be most valuable, and he has won many friends with his simple approach to the game of Cricket and the game of Life.

"I have studied the techniques of the great batsmen," says the cheerful Irish tinker. "And by plotting charts of their scoring areas against the most common field placings used by all the major County and international captains in various conditions, I have calculated that there are certain areas where I can score with reduced risk for increased reward."

LUMP

The unspoilt, jolly leprechaun warmed to his theme.

"I then worked out a method, using biomechanical models and geometrical diagrams regarding angle of bat, bat speed, position in the crease and various other factors to develop a technique at the crease which, if I may be forgiven for some self-aggrandisement, I believe to be among the most unique and effective in Cricket today."

How marvellous is Cricket that even a simple lump of unformed clay like this can share in her joys!

"Desperate"

Matters Of Lesser or Negligible Interest:

THIS PUBLICATION extends its condolences to the family of B.J. Turkleton, the former Notts off-spinner who has died, hideously, in Latin America. 'Gobbler', as he was known to all, was a keen ornithologist and had travelled to Peru to study the habits of its bird life. Sadly, he was bitten on his spinning finger by a parakeet, the digit swelling to the size of a small pumpkin before bursting and taking Gobbler's head clean off in the blast. He is survived by his wife and some children, and once took 8-35 against Lancashire on a batsman's wicket, including the hat-trick.

HER MAJESTY Queen Victoria, it is reported, has named her latest dachshund Timmy, in honour of the diminutive Warwickshire glovesman T.R. Ambrose. Her Majesty was said to be struck by the canine companion's shiny head and tiny feet and found the comparison highly suggestible, especially after watching Ambrose pouch six in the second innings at Hove v Sussex before attempting to bite fourth slip.

A MOST exciting opportunity for fans of the music hall should not be missed! A touring travelling family from Southern Africa, The Amazing Morkels, are soon to be embarking upon a tour of London and the Provinces. Binky, Bonky, Clyde, Snorkel and D'Brickashaw Morkel perform feats of tumbling, bicycle-play, acrobatics and useful hitting down the lower middle-order, and promise a diverting evening's merriment for all the family (no children).

THE POPULAR Kent opener R.W.T. Key will miss the first part of the English summer after an unfortunate over-eating incident.

THIS SECTION will no longer be sponsored by Sir Allen Roosterbender Stanford III Junior. It has emerged that Stanford, if that is indeed his real name, is little better than a common confidence trickster. Nothing whatsoever about his outward appearance gave any clue that Stanford might be unscrupulous. Readers should be assured: the publisher made every effort to verify Stanford's *bona fides* before accepting his money, and even considered drafting a letter politely enquiring if he was a criminal mastermind. What more due diligence could have been done?

The Eagerly Anticipated Conclusion Of The Indian Pre-Eminent League

Scenes of unprecedented exhilaration were witnessed at the Shillong Cricket Ground last month as the Assam Untouchables welcomed the Baluchistan Opium Exporters for the final of Mr Lalit Modi's estimable Twenty and Twenty cricketing extravaganza.

An excitable crowd were treated to a fearsome display of hitting from the Assam opening pair, especially their captain, D.L.F. Maximum. He struck 34 runs in just 97 deliveries, piercing the field again and again with wildly aggressive forward defensive strokes and stepping back in his crease to leave the ball with often reckless élan.

Just a few seasons ago, a total of 46 in only 20 overs could have existed only in the fevered imaginings of our most lurid shilling shocker authors, but Mr Modi has ensured that such devil-may-care batsmanship has become the norm. However, the Opium Exporters seemed listless in their reply, struggling to just 14 in their allocated overs and appearing unaware of the required rate.

The harum-scarum on the pitch as Mr Maximum made hay was matched by the cavorting of dancing girls alongside it, many of the local strumpetry clad in little more than full-length dresses and woollen hats.

One visiting member of MCC was violently sick at the spectacle, and questions are to be asked in the House about the wisdom of allowing the colonials to disport themselves in such a manner, unless Mr Modi offers a share of the purse.

TWENTY AND TWENTY MATCH BETWEEN ASSAM UNTOUCHABLES AND BALUCHISTAN OPIUM EXPORTERS, SHILLONG CRICKET GROUND

Assam Untouchables

DLF Maximum *	not out	34
MRF Blimp	not out	10
Extras (nb 2)		2
Total	(20 overs, without loss)	46

Baluchistan Opium Exporters

LA Reed	b Maximum	0
WS Burroughs II *	not out	3
S Vicious, Bt	b Blimp	8
EA Poe	not out	2
Extras (nb 1)		1
Total	(20 overs, for two)	14

Assam won by 32 runs; Baluchistan apparently confused by the match requirements. The Coutts Bank Occasion of Attainment was awarded to D.L.F. Maximum.

Eton Rifles v Working Men of Slough, The Playing Fields Of Eton

A spirited team of local players was routed by the young gentlemen of Eton College yesterday.

The Slough team, packed with lefties, was unable to contain the Eton attack, who unsettled their opponents with some disciplined braying before applying the coup de grâce and unleashing their polo ponies upon the visitors.

The Slough captain, P.J. Weller, attributed the opposition's powerful display to "all that rugby football putting hairs on their chest" and confessed, "we were no match for their untamed wit."

Fig. 1. 'Attack Ponies'

LETTER FROM OSCAR

EXTRACTED FROM MR WILDE'S COLLECTION OF WRITINGS ON CRICKET, 'A BATSMAN OF NO IMPORTANCE'. HERE, HE ADDRESSES MR BERNARD BOSANQUET, INVENTOR OF THE BEWILDERING 'GOOGLY'

The Savoy Hotel,
April 1895

My dearest Bosie,
Your sonnet was quite lovely, like sweet wine to me, as was the newspaper report of your six for 73 against Leicestershire. To read of those rough brutes groping in vain for your googlies was an exquisite joy. How I long to see again those strong and nimble fingers working away on the old ball like Apollo upon his lyre, as sure and swift now as they were when first I gazed upon you bewitching the Cambridge tailenders on The Parks during our Halcyon first summer together.

Alas, dear boy, my delightful memories of your wrong 'un may soon be all I have left. Against the wise counsel of my few remaining friends, I have challenged my enemies in court. I must travel this very day to Lord's to answer the MCC charge of corrupting the young by encouraging coltish tweakers such as yourself to bowl out of the back of the hand.

I beseech you not to intercede on my behalf, dear heart, and gain such comfort as you can from the sure knowledge that the delivery that dare not speak its name will one day be celebrated as the most exquisite form of sweet torment.

Your own,

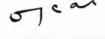

Being An Illuminating Intercourse With The Noted Australian Intellectual, Writer and Cricketer Mr Brett Lee

The exciting fair-haired Australian Mr Lee has enlivened many a cricket match with his rapid bowling, but it is in the field of applied moral philosophy that his greatest contributions to mankind's sum of achievements have come.

Had he not chosen to pursue glory upon the cricket field, it can be said without any doubt that Mr Lee would surely have a chair of philosophy at any of the great universities one could name, be it Oxford, The Sorbonne, Harvard or even The University Of G'day in Australia's Outback.

How would Mr Lee distil his philosophical studies, for the benefit of our readers?

"Aw look, mate," says the noted thinker. "I just give it my best shot, fair dinkum."

Mr Lee's title of the cleverest man in all Australia is well-earned.

Thank you, Mr Lee!

POINT, AND PERHAPS, COUNTER-POINT:

IS THE BARMINGTON ARMY MARCHING BAND A NUISANCE AT CRICKET?

PROPOSING:
HIS GRACE, THE BISHOP OF ROCHESTER

Our Lord Himself was known to be a keen games player ("And lo, He was thought to be dismissed but He did rise again and score a hundred before lunch in the second innings" from St Paul's Letter to the Marylebonites, 2:12).

And there is some theological evidence that He may have even been a spectator at early forms of sporting activity: "And it came to pass that He went into the Temple and sayeth to the crowd 'Let he who is without sin come and have a go if he thinks he be-eth hard enough, for verily I say unto him that he shall not make it to the station'" as recounted in Saint Danny of Dyer's Book of Punch-Ups, 1432.

But surely not even Our Lord, in His infinite patience, could sit through a day at The Oval listening to an ale-swilling group of 'supporters' shouting witlessly and playing the same song over and over again on the trumpet? The situation is becoming worse than Association Football!

RENOUNCING:
EBENEZER CATCHWEASEL,
PRESIDENT OF THE
BARMINGTON ARMY
MARCHING BAND

With the greatest of respect, His Grace should dismount from his altitudinous equine. The Barmington Army is merely a harmless diversion and our members have cheered the fellows on from Sandwich to Timbuktu. Many of us frequently dress as bishops, and indeed we count several prelates among our number.

I respectfully suggest that His Grace addresses me directly at the next match in which he is in attendance, and I shall be most happy to stow my trumpet in a vestibule of our mutual satisfaction, i.e. up his fundament.

OTHER NUISANCES AT CRICKET

Pigeons.

Hats.

Evolutionists.

THE WONDERFUL & MYSTERIOUS WORLD WHICH SURROUNDS US

A TREMENDOUSLY ENCOURAGING SOCIAL EXPERIMENT

It has long been the belief of this publication that Cricket can prove a most useful instrument in helping the lower orders to better themselves. And so it is with great pleasure that we report on the work of Mr Graham Gooch, whose exploits have been chronicled in a splendid recent stage play, *My Fair Batsman.*

"I was curious to see as to whether I could take a young lad from the ranks of the very poor and ill-educated, and train him in the arts of batsmanship, diction, moustache-grooming and being a good chap," says the estimable former Essex opening bat.

"But where was I to find the raw clay from which to mould my statue? I did not want a boy from a public school or one who had been coached by a club. I needed an untutored, entirely untouched youngster."

It was here that providence smiled upon Mr Gooch.

"I was taking a cab out from London through the East End to Essex, when it broke down in Forest Gate," he says. "It was the most damnable nuisance, because I had to get to Colchester in order to score a hundred against the touring Indians, and then head to my laboratory to work on my latest hair restoring concoction.

"While there, I observed some young urchins playing in the gutter with a stick and a ragged old ball. One boy caught my eye immediately.

"He was a cocksure little blighter, and no mistake," says Mr Gooch. "He struck a century and celebrated it in a most showy manner. Of course, his bat play was terribly raw, but I could tell that the seeds of considerable talent lay in this unpromising soil."

Mr Gooch immediately instructed the lad, R.S. Bopara, to accompany him to Essex, where he began a rigorous training programme to teach him not just the arts of batsmanship, but how to behave in a manner befitting a decent member of civilised society.

"One of my rivals in the field of hair restoration, the noted Australian Mr S.K. Warne, bet me a quite substantial sum that I could not make a cricketer out of the boy," says Mr Gooch. "Mr Warne was of the opinion that the lad did not have the right make-up."

Mr Gooch vowed to prove the Australian wrong.

"I had one of my most trusted boys, young Cook, take Bopara under his wing and teach him how to construct an innings without ever hitting the ball on the off; and show him how to sing descant on certain important choral works."

The young urchin quickly mastered many of the skills of batting, but it proved more difficult to teach him how to behave with decorum on the cricket field.

"He simply could not learn to respect the umpire's decision or do the correct, manly thing if he nicked one behind," says Mr Gooch sadly. "In one match, he was given out caught at the wicket and then shook his head, albeit imperceptibly, as he vacated the crease.

"I had to thrash him soundly and send him off to India to play Cricket there," says Mr Gooch. "This was something of a disaster. But I have not given up hope, and am convinced that I shall have my money from Mr Warne yet."

It is the fervent hope of this publication that Mr Gooch succeeds in his noble educational pursuit.

BEING AN ESPECIAL REPORT:

A MOST HEARTENING PROJECT INVOLVING THE YOUNG

Prostitution. Degradation. Drunkenness. Violence. Inequality. Syphilis.

A slum in the East End? The holiday of a Spaniard's dreams? The manifesto of the Fabian Society?

No. Sickening though it is to say, these evils are to be found in the dressing room of a leading County Cricket Club. Let the reader be under no illusion: the woes facing modern society are everywhere, and Cricket is not immune.

This reporter has witnessed County bowlers stupefied on opium. Promising young batsmen reduced to rag-clad waifs, begging for coins to spend on drink and linseed oil for their bats - or their thirsts. Senior professionals beating second eleven players with a stump. Even respected umpires carousing with women of the worst sort and contracting a dose of 'the lingering death'.

At the very moment our heroes join in manly battle with Australia on the fields of Lord's and Surrey and Trent Bridge, the dark underbelly

Fig. 1. Rev. M. Dotheboys. A keen interest in boys.

of County Cricket is spewing out fresh bile, the tragedy of squandered talent and incorrect left elbows.

Yet amid the gloom, a beacon of hope, like A.E. Stoddart among the murky mediocrity of the Middlesex middle-order. Thanks to the Reverend Merritt Dotheboys of Bromley-by-Bow, the next generation of cricketing youngsters may have been saved from the pipe, the public house and the prison.

The good vicar takes up the tale: "I was appalled by the

Fig. 2. Rev. Dotheboys' assistants, Steve and Eileen, display admirable humanity as they fish for fresh urchins on the Heath.

condition of the young cricketers in my parish. I organised games after Evensong in the local park, and found the boys underfed, runtish, listless and cowardly. They could scarcely field a firmly struck delivery or withstand a barrage of short stuff. Some lads as old as eight would wail and blub if hit in the face by the ball.

"It was saddening, and un-English, and un-Christian. But I vowed that, with God's help, I would change the future for the young cricketers of Bromley-by-Bow."

What happened next was, if the Reverend will forgive me, little short of a miracle.

"I began a good work that I christened the A Chance To Shine Foundation," explains the padre. "My plan was to take young boys who were slipping behind in the game of Cricket and the game of life, and give them some simple work to do, to build their confidence and educate them about the way of the world.

BALLS

"I knew Mr Thos Kooka-burringford, a local manufacturer of cricket balls, and he confided in me that he had a scheme to make his product the most sought-after in the land. But what he lacked was the

BEFORE   AFTER

cheap labour. This is where the A Chance To Shine Foundation came in."

Reverend Dotheboys put his youngsters to work in the cricket ball factory. Toiling in 31-hour shifts, they shone the cricket balls vigorously, using rags made of hessian dipped in mercury. This produced a uniquely deep and lasting sheen, enabling fast bowlers to carry on taking wickets well into their spells, and offering something for the twirlyman, too.

Demand for the new balls was vast, from Counties and Clubs alike.

"Mr Kookaburringford made a considerable sum from the venture," says the Reverend.

"And he was good enough to make a not insignificant cash donation to the Rectory Roof Restoration Fund.

"But the real winners were the young cricketers of Bromley-by-Bow," he adds. "The experience of working in the factory was invaluable. Many of the survivors swore to me they would practise hard at their Cricket day and night, and indeed several became professional players just to get out of the A Chance To Shine Foundation."

For the sake of Cricket, and England herself, one can only hope that there are more Reverend Dotheboys around the country.

Dr Grace's School for Cricket

Lesson Two: How To Catch
with guest lecturer Montgomery Panesar

Step 1. the Ball is still at some Distance
Estimating the angle of elevation, local barometric pressure and present wind speed and direction (if any), calculate the Ball's likely point d'aterrissage.

Step 2. the Ball's flight has reached its Apex
Appraise yourself of the relative positions of your fellow players. If Dr Grace is in the field, perhaps consider leaving the Ball for the better man. If Dr Grace is at bat, perhaps consider your future selection prospects.

Step 3. the Ball has begun its Descent
In a spirit of orderly and graceful haste, make your way towards the point in space where pitch and parabola will intersect, as determined in Step 1. Now may be the moment to summon a manservant if one is at hand.

Step 4. the Ball's proximity is no longer in Question
Have a stab at catching the fellow as he passes.

Step 5. the Ball has struck you; whereabouts now unknown
Maintain a studied insouciance while indicating the unfavourable position of the sun, or the unfavourable odour of nearby spectators should the day be overcast. Bandages may be applied discreetly once play resumes.

A Profound Investigation Into Matters Of The Utmost Importance:

The People Of The Abyss

A glorious evening at the Surrey Oval. The umpire calls stumps, the fine, manly fellows stride off, arm in arm, ruddy with the glow of the noblest of toils. Here comes the lion Richardson, looking as fresh as a daisy despite 30 overs - and six Hampshire wickets! - under his belt in the day. And here his brother in arms, the devastating Lockwood, trotting quickly off the field. The crowd cheers and whoops for their heroes, who smile shy but kind, their thoughts now on nothing but a wash and, I dare say, a pint of ale. The contemplation of yet another day's achievements may only come in their dotage, perhaps, but today belongs to the present and the young man. What a splendid sight to be in England, in her spring sunshine, the Empire stretching as far as man or savage eye can see: gentle land of plenty, of Queen Victoria, the right sort of Christianity, and Cricket.

And yet, a wretched smear befouls this Elysian field, as it does the whole country, like an unbroken puppy on a clean parlour floor. As Richardson strides off into the sanctity of the pavilion, three pathetic creatures emerge from its bowels. They seem half the size of the champion bowler, these men - if men they be. They slope onto the field of play, unable to meet his gaze, thin and shipwrecky next to the great

Fig. 1. Carbolic Acid can only do so much.

Fig. 2. Abyss-mal.

England hero. What can their purpose be? They are clad in a pathetic parody of cricketing gear - stained white trousers, worn through at the knee, shirts too big or too small, their shrunken, ant-like heads greasy and bare where a cap should be. I defy a man not to be moved to pity or horror by their listless, feeble foot movements or wheezing efforts as they begin to run in the field.

SKIRTS

Weep for them, Albion, these shadow men, these forgotten ghosts, these souls trapped in limbo: for these are the Second XI Players. Weep, gentle womenfolk, for these poor brutes; and brave men too, hang your heads at their un-capped pity. Not fine enough for the First XI, yet trapped by poverty, hopelessness and delusional, feverish imaginings of a glory that will never be, they cling on to Mother Cricket's skirts even as she kicks them firmly about the head and neck with the heavy boots of insufficient batting average and forces them to carry trays of lemonade to their thirsty betters.

STIFFS

The life of the Second XI player is one of endless, meaningless drudgery. Mowing the square with a pair of nail scissors. Bowling in the nets at the County's gentlemen members - and their prize for a wicket a fine of their paltry wages, or a sound thrashing with a stump. Lining the undergarments of the fast-bowling professionals with ham fat to prevent chafing. No indignity is too base for the Second XI 'stiff'.

These wretches eke out an existence on our fair land's cricket grounds from Cornwall to Northumbria, yet quite hopeless is their situation. I have spoken to players in Kent who are third generation Second XI wraiths; man passing on a cap-less penury to his son and he to his own lad. It is a beastly, shameful grotesquery of a Cricket life, and we are all diminished by it. Surely they must soon rise up, demand more County teams or smash the entire system itself. Or, at the very least, take up lawn tennis or the violin.

Ask Uncle Cricket!

BEING SOME KINDLY ADVICE
FOR THE YOUNG FELLOW
WHO IS DESIROUS OF
BECOMING AS PROFICIENT IN
THE ART OF BATSMANSHIP
AS THE SPLENDID
DR GRACE

Hello there, youngster! Hop up on Uncle Cricket's knee and we'll have a jolly old chat about the summer game.

What's that you say? What is that makes Dr Grace so fine and manly? Well, for a start, he wouldn't wail and blub like a girl just because an elder relative were to bowl him a few brisk ones with a hard ball on a rather treacherous surface such as the drawing room floor.

And I am quite certain that Dr Grace would not retire hurt simply because he had a slightly broken leg.

I think that is quite sufficient conversation for the time being. Now please go to your room and do not emerge until your leg has quite healed, or you have reached manhood's estate.

Your affectionate,
–*Uncle Cricket*

Some Wise Words From A Batsman Who Has 'Seen It All Before'

WE ASKED MR G. BOYCOTT OF YORKSHIRE HOW HE MEASURES SOME OF THE CRICKETING HEROES OF TODAY:

When I see some of these young bowlers today, I say to myself "I should fancy a bat against him!" When I played, it was against the likes of Sam Redgate and Alfred Mynn and let me tell you, they were most decidedly rapid. That was proper bowling, round-arm bowling, not this over-arm rubbish that we see today.

The bowlers today are not genuinely quick men such as I faced. When I first began to play at Cricket, it was against men like Edward 'Lumpy' Stevens. This lot that play now, they would not have enjoyed facing Lumpy much, let me tell you - he bowled underarm and you were lucky if you got through a session without a broken leg or being fatally struck about the temple by a delivery or two.

They have it easy, on their uncovered pitches, do the players these days. When I played, the pitch would be covered in glue and tar overnight, and have sharp rocks stuck into it and be ploughed with a harrow, while demonic creatures of the night performed their foul rituals on its surface. And I still played on it with a stick of rhubarb, and if the mood took me, I would wear my mother's pinafore while I did so.

FOR THE LADY

MRS DRAPER'S HELPFUL HANDBOOK FOR THE MODERN GENTLEWOMAN

To the lady of standing, no oversight, with the exception of giving voice to her foolish thoughts when the men are in discussion, could be more socially ruinous than incorrectly positioning the domestic staff at dinner.

Our s-x, in this matter as so many others, has a great deal to learn from our menfolk. We have already discussed how the sport of Cricket, although its more arcane laws may be too complex for our gentler intellects, has much to teach us about enduring bravely the frequent bouts of matrimonial duty that are womankind's eternal burden (see Number 17: Lie Back And Think Of England Gamely Battling Against The Follow-On v Australia at Sydney).

As in the bedroom, so in the dining room, and I urge you to commit this useful diagram to memory.

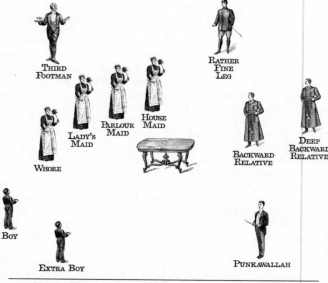

THIRD FOOTMAN

RATHER FINE LEG

LADY'S MAID

PARLOUR MAID

HOUSE MAID

WHORE

BACKWARD RELATIVE

DEEP BACKWARD RELATIVE

BOY

EXTRA BOY

PUNKAWALLAH

No. 23: The arrangement of servants at the dinner table

EDITOR'S NOTE

Our former Feminine Issues Correspondent, Mr William Babcock, has been dismissed from *The Wisden Cricketer's* employment after it was discovered that he was not, as he had previously claimed, a female.

Were it not for an eagle-eyed reader managing quite by happenstance to glance up Babcock's skirts as he rode the ascending 'moving escalator' at Mr Harrod's Brompton Road department store, the creature might have continued in his unmanly, or rather unwomanly, subterfuge indefinitely.

Our gratitude is due to Rev. J. Wilson of Godalming, who receives a magnificent bat signed by the Surrey First XI for his troubles. Babcock has been replaced by Mrs Draper, who is

Mrs Draper: Accommodating

a splendidly womanly person and well-known to many of the chaps on the County circuit.

Cricket lovers all over the Empire must be ever-vigilant of men in women's attire, especially our readers in the Far East and those at the lesser public schools.

WOMEN BAKERS OF ENGLAND!

APPLICATIONS ARE BEING TAKEN FOR CAKES TO BE DELIVERED TO THE TEST MATCH SPECIAL BOX. PRECEDENCE WILL BE GIVEN TO CAKES WITH: AMUSING SUGAR ICING IN THE SHAPE OF AN ANATOMICAL PART; CAKES WITH BRANDY IN; CAKES WITH POWERFUL OPIATES IN.

THE PAVILION OF HORRORS

OUR BLOODY SERIAL CONTINUES...

Our last instalment saw plucky cricket-loving Lord's skivvy Eliza discover that her hero, the MCC's celebrated left-handed bat J.T. 'Johnny' Brawnston-Smyth, is engaged to be married to a vampire – and one who feeds her diabolic lust for blood on members of the St John's Wood groundstaff, at that!

The rest of the day passed in a blur. Twice Eliza caught the sharp end of Mrs Mordeth's tongue - as if there was another end! - for not working quickly enough. As punishment, she was sent to bring Major Tuppington his afternoon tea. The oldest member always partook of a foul-smelling concoction of curried egg in gin (a legacy of his time in India, it was said) at four o'clock in the library.

The Major had been a wicketkeeper of some renown in his youth, but now his 'quick hands' were employed in altogether more beastly manners, primarily the molestation of whichever girl was unfortunate enough to come within bail-whipping distance of his armchair.

But today, Eliza scarcely cared, for her head was spinning with what she had just seen. Did Johnny know that Miss Wellington was a vampire? Was he himself a vampire? Surely not - Eliza refused to believe that any man who could play so beautifully off the back foot could be a creature of the night. If not, then she must save Johnny from the clutches of his blood-thirsty betrothed. Quite evidently, extreme caution was needed - and more knowledge of her enemy.

Side-stepping the Major's lunge like the nimble-footed Ranji playing the leg-break, she delivered his vile meal and, checking nobody sentient was around, scanned the shelves for anything that might provide some clue. The books' titles were bewildering to a girl of Eliza's modest erudition - she had left school at the age of three to work in the asbestos factory - but she steeled herself with thoughts of Johnny.

'Cricket And The Occult in Prep Schools'... 'Lycanthropes And Leg-Spinners'... 'David Frith on The Great Medium Pacers Of Hades'... This was no use! Just as she despaired, Eliza saw a small, tattered volume entitled 'Vampyres And The Correct Way To Play Them'. She glanced around the room: the members were either asleep, dribbling or drinking heavily, and in many cases all three. She pouched the book in her pinny.

Secluded in a cupboard under the Pavilion's main stair, Eliza read in breathless wonder. It was immediately clear that Miss Wellington was a vampire as described in the book, which alluded to "the olde relationshippe between the noble game of crickette and the undeade". Worse, the book told of Cricketing Vampyres - the most dangerous of all their bloodsucking kind - creatures that slept under the turf of their home County, and could come out, if not into direct sunlight, then certainly into overcast and swing-friendly conditions. They did not take lunch, but often hunted during the tea interval, picking off drunken spectators with ease. The females were known to attach themselves to notable cricketers, particularly top-order batsmen, with a view to biting them and creating Vampire Cricket Lovers for themselves in eternity. The book suggested that many of the great Hambledon teams of the last century were made up entirely of vampires, condemned to travel the country beating all-comers and feeding defeated opponents to their diabolical wives.

Eliza snapped the book shut in alarm. She must try to warn Johnny. But how could she possibly approach him with this? Scuttling back to the scullery, she saw Peg, a fellow dogsbody at the Pavilion, and her only friend at Lord's. She pulled Peg into an alcove. Peg gawped.

"Peg: I've discovered something about Johnny - Mr Brawnston-Smyth, I mean. I think he may be in mortal peril."

Peg was a sweet girl, gentle and kind, but she was not the sharpest slip in the cordon. She stared at Eliza with her mouth open for a few seconds.

"No, he's in the dressing room," she said. "I seen him go in."

"No, no. Peril. Danger. Trouble. I think Miss Wellington wants to drink his blood."

"Was she not give a cup of tea when she come in, then?" asked Peg. "Because there'll be 'ell to pay from Mordeth if she's not 'ad a cup of tea."

"Listen," said Eliza, growing impatient. "Miss Wellington is a vampire, and she plans to drink Johnny's blood and turn him into a vampire too and I have to save him because I love him, Peg, I love everything about him from his hair to his arms to his attractive dabs through point."

Peg stared thoughtfully in silence. For some time.

"Peg?"

"Oh, sorry, 'liza," she said. "Just drifted away there. Well, we best go warn Mr Brawnston-Smyth, ain't we?"

The brave, dear girl grabbed Eliza's slender little hand in her rather chubby paw, and marched her upstairs to the dressing rooms. It was risky indeed to enter the gentlemen's rooms, but Peg had the fearlessness that comes from a big heart and the brain-power of a crustacean. She was just about to knock when they both froze at a familiar yell.

"Eliza Tanner! Come here this minute."

It was Mrs Mordeth. She was up a ladder to dust a portrait of C.B. Fry wrestling a tiger while batting against Australia, one of the most valuable paintings in all of Lord's and only to be cleaned by the most senior staff.

"Go and get me a fresh cloth from downstairs," she said. "And don't drag them big feet of yours."

Eliza's heart sank, but as she walked off she saw that Peg, with a wink, had slipped into the dressing room as Mrs Mordeth turned away. Kind, brave Peg! Eliza fairly skipped downstairs to get the cloth.

When she came back up the

stairs, Mrs Mordeth, strangely, was nowhere to be seen. And nor was Peg, yet the dressing room door was wide open. Puzzled, Eliza peeked around the edge. There seemed to be nobody inside. This was good! Perhaps she could leave Johnny an anonymous note. Yes! That was it. Quickly, she nipped inside and closed the door.

Eliza froze. Her knees buckled. A silent scream came from her dry throat.

Poor Peg - poor sweet, silly, unthinking Peg - hung from one of the hooks on the wall, with bite marks in her neck, her throat torn out, a horrible fixed grin on her face and her blood pooling below in a cricket bag belonging to the nuggety opener R.F. Jackson, who always favoured the leg-side and had a well-known fondness for the pull-shot.

Eliza began to sob. She heard the door close behind her. She turned.

"You couldn't keep your mouth shut, could you?" said Mrs Mordeth. "Now what are we to do with you?"

To Be Continued...

WHAT FATE WILL BEFALL POOR ELIZA AT THE HANDS OF THE EVIL MRS MORDETH? WHO ELSE AT LORD'S IS INVOLVED IN THE VAMPIRE CARRY-ON? WHAT EFFECT WILL ALL THIS HAVE ON THE OUTCOME OF THE IMPORTANT CLASH WITH YORKSHIRE? DO NOT FAIL TO PURCHASE THE NEXT EDITION OF THE WISDEN CRICKETER TO DISCOVER MORE ABOUT THE PAVILION OF HORRORS!

Also In The Forthcoming Issue!

ACCEPT NO SUBSTITUTES
OR REPLACEMENTS

Scientific experiment to discover if a cricketer can outrun a bear... The scourge of corruption: was Boer War fixed?... Wildlife and obituaries... An arousing and confusing picture of a female in cricketing garb... Should the Irish be allowed to play Cricket?... An interview with a leading photomaniac on the fascinating business of cricketing photography... Ought smoking to be banned in the slips?... Beards and the medium pace bowler... Mr S.K. Warne on Miss Florence Nightingale...

BOOK REVIEWS

FROM OUR ESTEEMED
LITERATURE AND CAT-
RACING CORRESPONDENT,
MONTGOMERY 'INKY'
PATTERSON

NO BOUNDARIES

BY MR RONALD IRANI

Mr Irani, as readers will of course be aware, fashioned for himself a career as a dogged but limited right-handed bat and medium-pace bowler for Essex. It is to our nation's considerable shame that Mr Irani was selected for the touring party of Rhodesia two summers ago, where a team lead by M.A. 'Dirtypocket' Atherton somehow neglected to beat the natives, many of whom had never played Cricket before, and at least some of whom had to miss entire days' play in order to attend to their chickens. As suggested by the title of his book, Mr Irani is a quite deranged and dangerous socialist who seeks nothing less than the total abolishment of nation-statehood and a loose internationalist coalition of workers' co-operatives. His views are as sickening as his prose, and indeed his medium-paced bowling, and should be avoided like the plague. This is why I was careful to burn this book without reading it, as should you. His forays into 'broadcasting' his convictions on the newfangled 'wireless radio' are merely sad.

Mr Irani – Crazed.

Out Of My Comfort Zone

by Mr Stephen Waugh

This is a deeply disturbing erotic novella detailing an Australian gentleman's powerful, obsessive love of all things English and his attendant self-loathing at his own misfortune in being born in the aforementioned colony. It should be read with caution, and ideally a glass of Armagnac, better to calm the nerves after a particularly visceral early passage about his 'baggy green'. Out of courtesy to our lady readers and members of the clergy, I shall say no more.

Please Do Not Be So Presumptuous As To Appraise Kath Of These Matters Herein Discussed

by Mr Ian Terrence Botham

Without question the greatest single work of English literature since *Beowulf*.

MRS CECILY BEASTING GUIDES YOU THROUGH MATTERS OF CRICKET, CORRECTNESS AND THE HEART...

Dear Mrs Beasting,

I quite often attend matches involving Warwickshire County Cricket Club. I find the sight of their fair-haired middle-order bat, I.R. Bell, drives me quite to distraction. Would it be beyond the pale to take to the field and wring the little blighter's neck?

–*Major R. Dickson,*
Leamington Spa

Dear Major,

On the contrary, this might be exactly what the individual in question needs in order to make a man of him. Or it may scar him for the rest of his life. Either way, you will derive considerable satisfaction from the assault, and should attempt to throttle the elegant right-hander with neither delay nor compunction.

Yours,
–*Mrs Cecily Beasting*

Dear Mrs Beasting,

I suffered a most unconscionably embarrassing episode recently during a Cricket match on Frampton Green. My husband was playing for Old

Radleians against the local chaps, and had the misfortune to be fatally struck on the head while fielding at cover. I must confess I allowed my emotions to quite get the better of me and ran onto the field of play without my parasol. Of course, everybody was extremely kind, and affected not to notice my lapse in decorum. However, I am mortified at this wanton display of emotion and breach of protocol. Mrs Beasting, I beseech you: is there any way to make amends?

—*Mrs Caroline Frobisher, Stonehouse*

Dear Mrs Frobisher,

I regret to inform you that the situation is quite hopeless. The best advice I can offer you is to take your own life with as little fuss as possible.

With best wishes,
—*Mrs Cecily Beasting*

Dear Mrs Beasting,

Last summer, I attended a garden party where a most diverting game of French cricket took place involving members of both sexes. I must confess to you, Mrs Beasting, that the spectacle of the flower of young English womanhood, its skirts hitched up fully two inches above the ankle, bent over just very slightly, sticking its tongue out of the corner of its mouth as it furrowed its brow in concentration to receive the slippery, spitting delivery...
(Letter truncated due to considerations of space —Ed.)

Dear Reverend Potterweevil,

Your query is indecent and quite beastly. I have no wish to discuss summer parties at my own home with you, much less the possibility or otherwise of French play in my private garden. As to your suggestion of frolicking down by my ha-ha, I must insist that you write with further, precise details at the earliest opportunity, to better allow me to dispense the correct advice.

—*C.B.*

DISCREET SEAMSTRESS

BALLS TAMPERED
STITCHING RAISED
NO QUESTIONS ASKED

Box 222, Oakham

FACTS ABOUT
C.B. FRY

Mr C.B. Fry has recently turned his hand to invention, and has patented or discovered: the pneumatic hammer; the 'zipper' fastening device; colour photography; the carburettor; the wireless radio; and the iPad, a type of slate tablet useful for striking a recalcitrant domestic servant.

Mr C.B. Fry can perform astonishing feats of memory and has memorised the names and ages of every man living in Leicestershire, as well as most of the women, and a good portion of the farm animals.

Mr C.B. Fry is the possessor of the longest big toe in First Class Cricket: his left. Curiously, his right big toe is of only median length.

Mr C.B. Fry is quite a clever pianist, but finds it uncomfortable to play after an argument with the Sultan of Turkey over the correct phrasing in a Chopin prelude. The Sultan slammed C.B. Fry's fingers in the lid of a Steinway, but C.B. Fry countered by deposing the spiteful Turk and installing a puppet ruler in his place.

Mr C.B. Fry once held the Swedish middleweight jujitsu title, but lost in a heavily disputed split decision to Sven 'The Eel' Natamaka and refused to compete again.

Mr C.B. Fry once grew the largest marrow in all Carmarthenshire. He lists it among his proudest achievements.

A 24-Hour Period In The Daily Existence Of...

K.P. Pietersen

BEING HIS DAILY DISCIPLINES AND DIVERSIONS

SIX O'CLOCK...

I rise early and breakfast on a most refreshing sup of Mr Rackham Bull's Red Bull energetic facilitation concoction, a product which I am only too happy to endorse but one I should consume personally nevertheless. It is said to give you wings and I am not one to argue!

EIGHT O'CLOCK...

My wife, the noted music hall entertainer Miss Jessica of Liberatum X, and myself promenade throughout the capital, perhaps purchasing some of the latest most fashionable clothing and endeavouring to get noticed in all the right places.

ELEVEN O'CLOCK...

The real business of the day begins for Kevin Pietersen: staring into the looking glass practising his cricketing shots and generally admiring his personage.

THREE O'CLOCK...

Invent a new type of cricketing shot.

FOUR O'CLOCK...

To the netting facilities, where I work assiduously on my new shot, repeatedly getting out.

FIVE O'CLOCK...

Rehearse defiant insistences to the gentlemen of the press that I shall continue to play the new shot, despite its obviously disastrous consequences.

EIGHT O'CLOCK...

Early to bed to work on my memoirs and practise referring to myself in the third person. Good night from Kevin Pietersen, admirers!

Mr Pietersen invents another pointless shot

74

Autumn 1896
— The Ashes —

THE
WISDEN
CRICKETER

VOL. I - No 3   AUTUMN 1896   PRICE ONE PENNY

The sun at his zenith, Her Majesty on the throne and the Australians here in Albion to do battle for those Ashes. What more thrilling August activity could an Englishman dream of, with the possible exception of seeing a lady's ankles at the seaside or violently subduing the native population of somewhere hot and beastly?

Our Ashes edition offers the reader an opportunity to learn more about England's heroes, marvel at the successful 'motorised omnibus' parade undertaken by the victors through the capital, and glean some important travel advice prior to the rematch 'Down Under' next winter, for which purpose the first steamships are already leaving Southampton.

With such a cornucopia of amusements in store, I shall take up no more of your time, dear reader, other than to say what a rare honour it is to be appointed the third editor (acting) of this magazine, and fervently to hope that my tenure is longer than that of my unfortunate predecessor. I pray that, in time, society will judge Bartholomew Shipman more kindly than did the magistrate at Winchester Crown Court. It is my own opinion that those nuns overreacted quite hysterically, and that Mr Shipman might very well have been up that ladder outside their bedroom window for the purposes of swatting a bee. Cricketing journalism's loss is, without doubt, Her Majesty's Penal System's gain.

—Roderick Jarndyce,
Acting Editor

CORRESPONDENCE
(NO CORRESPONDENCE WILL BE ENTERED INTO)

SIR, There has been much praise of the so-called sporting behaviour of England's premier all-rounder in commiserating with his defeated Australian opponent during the fiercely contested recent Ashes series. If I were Dr Grace, I should check my pocket watch and wallet, for the Australian bowler will almost surely have swiped the items during the aforementioned handshake of consolation. Their ways are not our ways, and they cannot help themselves but to purloin and pilfer wherever possible.
—*P.C. Lewis, Bow Street*

SIR, The number of foreign players in the English team has gone beyond a joke. I have it on very good authority that the bowler, Lohmann, has a great aunt who is suspected of being Welsh. And this Ranji fellow, well, he may play his Cricket at Hove, but I strongly suspect the chap might be from anywhere as far away as Hastings or possibly even Suffolk.
—*Mrs N.J. Griffin,*
England

SIR, In the recent Ashes series, the Australian bowler E. Jones propelled the ball through Dr Grace's beard. It is frightening to think of the injuries England's captain might have sustained had he been clean-shaven. And yet still there are those who argue against the entirely sensible Act of Parliament insisting that all First Class cricketers should have a full beard, or at the very least an extravagant set of moustaches. I sometimes think these dissenters will not be happy until a fresh-faced youth is killed at the wicket and we are all as smooth-faced as the worst sort of continental catamite.
—*Mr G. Beard,*
Sideburn-on-the-Naze

OFF HIS TROLLEY-BUS!

UNSTEADY FREDDIE TOASTS ASHES VICTORY

AN EXCITING ACCOUNT OF THE ENGLAND CRICKET TEAM'S SPLENDID PROCESSION THROUGH LONDON, INCLUDING REPORTS OF A THRILLING NEW TYPE OF VEHICLE AND AN INCIDENT OF PUBLIC DRUNKENNESS

Great scenes were witnessed in the capital last week as the England cricket team, fresh from an Ashes triumph over Australia, toured the city in a 'motorised omnibus'.

Leading the celebrations was the popular all-rounder and inebriation artist Mr 'Fat' Freddie Flintstone.

The victorious XI were driven around London in the latest engine-powered transport from the clever German Herr Karl Benz.

Herr Benz's omnibus is said to be able to travel at the indecent speed of fully nine (9) miles in the hour. Fortunately, on this occasion, the vehicle was kept to a more respectable two miles in the hour, on account of not wishing to alarm any ladies present in the crowd, and because Flintstone kept falling off it.

"A few drinks"

The procession began in Greenwich, where a small fire was started in the Royal Observatory when Flintstone attempted to light a cigar by focusing the sun's rays through the large telescope therein, before the omnibus made its erratic way

Fig. 1. How the 'Omnibus' may, or may not, have looked.

into London herself.

The cricketing heroes were awarded The Most Honourable Order Of The Bath by Her Majesty at Buckingham Palace, even those who had played only one of the matches or were drawn from the ranks of the lower orders.

There was a brief tour around Hyde Park, where Flintstone contrived to fall into The Serpentine and consume several of Her Majesty's swans, before the team attended a reception at Downing Street.

There was some confusion when a few less-educated members of the eleven - i.e. players from The North - appeared to think that, rather than meeting the Prime Minister Mr Gladstone, they were in fact "going for a few drinks with Gladstone Small".

The neck-deficient former Warwickshire bowler was not involved in the festivities.

Lesser Items of Topical Note:

CONGRATULATIONS are due to the Australian batsman D.C. Boon, who has broken one of the most prestigious records in Australian sport. On the recent steamship voyage from Sydney to Southampton, Mr Boon consumed no fewer than 1,452 bottles of port wine. The previous holder, R.W. Marsh, had imbibed 1,437 bottles on the long journey, claiming he "could have had a few more, but did not want to set a bad example to the younger fellows".

THE LEADERS of the burgeoning 'nationalism' movement in Australia have seen fit to issue a 'Declaration' that elucidates the ten key tenets of what they describe as 'Australianism'. These are:
– The right to bear sheep.
– The right to shear sheep.
– Never walking even when out.
– The importance of being a good bloke, mate and cobber.
– All men being created equal (apart from foreigners, pooftahs, etc).
– Never using a nightwatchman.
– Not liking Pommies.
– Compulsory moustaches for all adult males. Optional moustaches for all adult females.

THE POLICE and concerned zoological experts are appealing for information from any persons who may have seen the escaped Ponting's Monkey, which somehow broke free from its enclosure at London Zoo last month. It is prone to running erratically and can become easily moved to anger if challenged or hindered during a run.

KEITH scores a century before lunch v Notts; remanded for common assault during interval.

THE NOTED cardsharp, swordsman and gourmand, Mr Shane Warne, will be at Bottley's Apothecary in Covent Garden each Wednesday in the month of October demonstrating the miraculous effects of his latest patented hair restorer and diuretic concoction.

Shamed By Your Mistakes In English?
Good.

Was this the finest series in the history of Test Cricket?

The 1896 Ashes, in which England triumphed over Australia by a scoreline of 2-1, will be remembered as long as the game is played, not just for the quality of the Cricket, but the manner in which it was contested.

In this, typically, England took the example of their captain, W.G. At Old Trafford, the Australian opening bowler Harry Trott sent down a delivery that struck Dr Grace plumb on the front pad, before hitting his bat and crashing into the stumps, knocking over all three. The ball was then caught by the Australian wicket-keeper, Kelly, who stumped Dr Grace for good measure.

Undaunted, the never-say-die Gloucestershire medic set off for a single, at which Kelly threw down the stumps at the bowler's end, adding run-out to stumped, bowled, caught and leg before. After only 20 minutes of shouting and remonstrating furiously with the umpire, threatening to cancel the match and "have [his] friends in the Navy invade your Godforsaken little country", W.G. walked off without a murmur, pausing only to hit deep fine leg with his shooting stick and personally fine the tourists 150 per cent of their match fees.

No doubt a continental or a footballer would have over-reacted quite childishly. Such is the sportsmanship that sets the greatest game, and the Englishman, apart from the rest!

OUR ASHES HEROES!

MR KRAAL P. PIETERSEN
Rescued from certain obscurity at the hands of Natives in the Cape Colony, Pietersen enjoys sugary drinks, inventing new cricketing shots and admiring his own reflection in a highly-polished piece of tin that he keeps especially for the purpose.

MR ARBUTHNOT STRAUSS
Has drawn warm praise for his expansive drives, both through the off-side and those approaching the front entrance of his family seat.

MR SILAS BROAD (NÉE MISS AMELIA BLENNERHASSET)
Beyond question one of the most talented young cricketers ever to undergo gender reassignment surgery.

OUR ASHES HEROES!

MR AUGUSTUS J. ANDERSON
*Although beset by injury to the back earlier in his career,
the Burnley man has seen immeasurable improvements
since wearing a whalebone corset for bowling.*

MR TITUS P. COLLINGWOOD
*When not playing Cricket, Colling-
wood enjoys a round of golf, talking
about golf, thinking about golf or
hiding on the golf links in a bunker
in the hopes of seeing further golf.*

MR AGATHA COOK
*Discovered by the noted battingolo-
gist Mr G.A. Gooch in a Bedford-
shire sprout farm, young Cook is
widely expected to captain either
England or the choir of St George's
Chapel, Windsor.*

English XI Effect Glorious Triumph Over Dastardly Band of Bloodthirsty Desperadoes

The honour of Queen and Country was upheld last month in The North when Lord Sheffield's XI achieved a most splendid victory against a highly dangerous Convict XI, who wore balls and chains throughout for the safety of the home team and its attendant womenfolk.

The criminals, shipped over especially for the purpose, were lead by their captain G.K. Warne (deported for stealing a mutton pie) and their fast men W.P. McGrath (28 years hard labour for cheeking a constable) and D.D. Siddle (deported for having red hair). The villains made a moderately impressive start, with the last-named ruffian clean-bowling his Lordship through the gate (fortuitously).

Fig. 1. Justice!

However, the convicts' lack of moral fibre soon began to tell and they proved quite unable to match the mettle of eleven honest Englishmen playing hard and true, nor master their manacled limbs.

CONVICTS OF TASMANIA XI V LORD SHEFFIELD'S XI
LORD SHEFFIELD'S FRONT LAWN, SHEFFIELD
5, 6, 7 JULY 1896 (THREE-DAY MATCH)

Lord Sheffield's XI 1st Innings

Lord Sheffield *	b Siddle	0
WG Denholm-Elliott	b McGrath	276
PP Pinkington-Pink	not out	204
FE Manlove	not out	102
Extras (b 96, lb 24, nb 1)	....	121
Total	(for 3 wickets, declared) ..	703

Convicts of Tasmania XI 1st Innings

GK Warne *	run out	0
B Johnson	run out	4
PF Border	run out	6
WB Lee	run out	16
C Clark	run out	0
K Clarke	run out	0
ST Waugh	run out	0
FR Marsh †	run out	12
WP McGrath	run out	6
PWC Hughes	run out	4
DD Siddle	run out	0
Extras (b 3, nb 2)	....	5
Total	(all out, 26.1 overs)	53

Convicts of Tasmania XI 2nd Innings (following on)

GK Warne *	run out	0
B Johnson	run out	4
PF Border	retired hurt	
WB Lee	retired exhausted	
C Clark	retired shot	
K Clarke	retired dead	
ST Waugh	retired pardoned	
FR Marsh †	retired flogged	
WP McGrath	retired to pub	
PWC Hughes	absent	
DD Siddle	unknown	
Extras (b 5, nb 2)	....	7
Total	(all out, 1.1 overs)........	11

Lord Sheffield's XI won by an innings and 639 runs.

An Interesting Insight Into The Methods Of The England 'Coaching Supervisor', By Mr Andrew Flower

On the day of an important match, I almost never encourage the fellows to fiddle about in the nets or work at Cricket.

It pains me to say so, but the England team tend toward mental feebleness. Given their only limited powers of concentration, I find it more efficacious to keep their minds off Cricket until the actual game commences.

As such, I will have them ready themselves for the day with a short game of association football, or perhaps play under the rugger code, depending on the number of fellows from Southern Africa in the team on that day.

After that, we practise at quoits, tumbling, tennis, shove ha'penny and various forms of Oriental martial art, usually culminating in a vigorous bout of stick-fighting to blow off some steam.

If a match is of particular import, we will complete our preparations with a brisk cavalry charge, using fixed bayonets and live munitions (see Figure 1).

Of course, scarcely a session goes by without one of the

Fig. 1. More invigorating than blocking a few in the nets

fellows sustaining some sort of serious injury, and it would be remiss of me to deny that there has been the odd fatality in the 'warm-up'.

However, with an almost limitless supply of players from the Cape to call upon, I don't see why we should not have a little fun while we're about it.

BEING AN ILLUMINATING INTERCOURSE WITH S.C.G. MACGILL

It is a truth universally acknowledged, that an Australian in possession of a good fortune, must be in want of a drink.

The opinion the right-thinking Englishman has of his colonial cousin from 'Down Under' is that of a drunken, boorish brute with no more grasp of culture or sophisticated matters than a Nottinghamshire miner has upon the basics of personal hygiene.

Of course, this is almost entirely true. However, there are exceptions to the rule, such as the leg-spinning marvel Mr Stuart MacGill, reportedly the most refined and intellectual Australian as ever drew breath.

Is it true, this publication asked MacGill, that he not only enjoys wine, but that he has even been known to drink from a glass, rather than straight from the bottle in the traditional Australian manner?

"It is," confirmed MacGill.

Emboldened, although not without some reservations, your interviewer then asked Mr MacGill to confirm that he has, on occasion, been known to read a book - and not one about criminal techniques, nor under duress, neither.

"Yes," said this unique Antipodean. He elaborated further:

"That is why they slung me out the cricket team."

POINT, AND POSSIBLY,
COUNTER-POINT:

SHOULD A BATSMAN 'WALK' IF HE KNOWS THAT HE IS OUT?

PROPOSING:
FATHER PETER JOHN
CORMACK GILCHRIST,
PADRE OF THE FOURTH
ROYAL IRISH DRAGOON
GUARDS, ENTHUSIASTIC
RECREATIONAL UMPIRE
AND STUDENT OF THE
LIVES OF THE SAINTS

Who among us in his time has not been struck on the front pad of human frailty by one that nips back, or feathered one behind off the outside edge of wickedness, and thought to himself: "If I keep my own counsel here, I may yet be given not out"? And, indeed, sometimes one may survive. But at what cost?

I ask all betempted batsmen to remember the blessed Ignatius of Antioch, one of the earliest of the Christian martyrs - and, incidentally, the first of the left-handed Saints to experiment with an off-stump guard to counter the slanted delivery. Ignatius was a patient opening bat whose greatest, and final, innings came in a heroic rearguard against the Emperor Trajan on a drying wicket in the Flavian Amphitheatre (AD 108). With the light fading, Trajan sent down a brutish lifter that brushed Ignatius on the glove on the way through. The umpire was unmoved, so the furious Trajan brought on his lions. The Bishop knew what he must do: he tucked his bat under his left arm and his bishopric mace under his right, and walked off. On his way to the pavilion, he was eaten by the lions, but he died in the Light of the Lord and having followed not just the Letter but the Spirit of the Game.

Truly he is with God now, as is each of us when he commends his wicket to the love of the Lord and walks without waiting for the finger of mortal judgement, whose offices shall fade away like dust or the Essex lower-middle order on a turning pitch.

RENOUNCING:
DOCTOR H.M. WAUGH,
EMERITUS PROFESSOR
OF APPLIED MORAL
DIALECTICS AT THE
UNIVERSITY OF SYDNEY,
PHILOSOPHER AND
RESOLUTE MIDDLE-ORDER
BATSMAN

Walk? Not bloody likely.

Bowden's Umpiring Field Guides – Vol. XIII
Newly Updated & Revised, including: 'The Dangers Of Revealing Arcane Secrets Of International Conspiracies' & 'Standing for Long Periods With Two Broken Legs'.

THE WONDERFUL & MYSTERIOUS WORLD WHICH SURROUNDS US

BUSHCRAFT

BEING A STUDY OF THE WAYS IN WHICH THE AUSTRALIAN CRICKET SPECTATOR NAVIGATES USING NATURE'S BOUNTY AND OTHER INGENIOUS MEANS

English visitors to Australia this winter would be well advised to take heed of the meritoriously clever ways in which the native cricketing enthusiast finds his way around this large and inhospitable country.

Myriad are the challenges facing the traveller, from dangerous wild animals to risibly confusing place names, from wanton bearded ladies to men in the outback hell-bent on murdering the tourist and his female companion.

So how does the Australian Cricket spectator himself stand up to these challenges?

Well, happily, the Australian is above all a simple soul. If he can find his way from the public house to the sporting arena via the sheep-shearing station and the dunny, the name by which he shamelessly refers to the W-ter Cl-set, the Australian considers his day well spent.

If he can do it without falling down dead drunk, losing all his money on an 'automatic poker machine', chanting obscenely for six hours or getting roped in to an impromptu recital on the wobbleboard with some of his cousins, so much the better.

Sadly, the vast size of the country, its debilitating heat and the Australian's insatiable genetic predisposition towards crime and public indecency make even the simplest daily journey problematic.

It is with this reason that the Cricket enthusiast from 'Down Under' has invented a clever system of tracking and marking to remind himself of the route to and from the cricket ground.

He may fashion a small wicket with discarded beer bottles to signal to other wanderers that Cricket is played to a decent level nearby.

He may trim a eucalyptus tree into the shape of a moustache to indicate that a gritty, counterpunching number three batsman is to be found in the area.

He may even scratch obscene and wicked words into the turf with his boot to indicate that

STUDIES IN BUSHCRAFT

The Wisden Cricketer wishes to thank Dr Oswald Bonzer for permission to reprint the following examples, extracted from his excellent tome 'Australian Stone Circles: Secret Aboriginal Messages Or Just A Pile Of Dingo Turds?'

(A) ARCANO-STUMPERY – INDICATING HIDDEN PERILS TO OTHERS THROUGH THE ARRANGEMENT OF WOODEN STICKS

All Clear   *Proceed With Care*   *Crikey! This one's a bit lively*   *Pray For Rain*

(B) DIPSO-DOWSOLOGY – EXAMINING MARKINGS ON THE GROUND IN ORDER TO LOCATE NATURAL SOURCES OF REFRESHMENT IN THE PARCHED EARTH OF THE OUTBACK

Dry River Bed. No water present.   *Dry Martini. Indian Tonic Water also likely.*   *Dry Sherry. Watering Hole within 6 yards*

a competitive Australian seam bowler has been sighted in the vicinity.

With these homely expedients does the Australian spectator conquer his environment.

In lieu of literature, music, arts, philosophy and basic table manners, the visitor to Australia should salute this unparalleled national cultural achievement and learn from it.

TRAVEL WITH TUFFERS

RENOWNED BALLROOM DANCER, EXPLORER AND HERBALIST
P.C.R. TUFNELLTON FURNISHES SEVERAL NOTABLE
RECOMMENDATIONS FOR YOUR AUSTRALIAN ADVENTURE

FLORA & FAUNA

Less fecund than our own blessed land, the Outback requires a firm and masterful hand before she yields her moist bounty. Here then, Mr Tufnellton peruses some of the plants indigenous to Australia and the effects that may be achieved by smoking, eating or inserting them into one's person...

LEAFIUS LEAFIUS
Green. Or possibly brown.

LEAFIUS LAFFIUS
Definitely green, this one.

LEAFIUS LOOFIUS
Blue?

LEAFIUS BIGGIUS
Hmmm. Pass.

LEAFIUS EATIUS
Found this little fella in me salad.

LEAFIUS PUFFIUS
Good Gear.

Sartorial Safety

Upon arrival in the Colony, it is suggested that you adopt the appearance of one of the natives in order to bamboozle and disorientate pick-pockets, brigands, highwaymen etc., of which Australia is, it hardly needs saying, peerlessly well-stocked.

Transforming From Gentleman to Australian
On the left, adroit. On the right, a gauche.

Useful Phrases

Patois	*Translation*
Eight for two	Two for eight
Three for five	Five for three
Ten to two	Ten to six (GMT)
I never even nicked it	I am out
We play hard but fair	I'd sell my own granny for a caught behind
We'll all have a beer together later	I will kill you in your sleep

A Somewhat Noteworthy Investigation:

The Sickening Indignities That Await The Cricketer Upon Retirement

*"What becomes of those for whom Cricket has
no further use, mama?"*
*"The poor wretches must become light entertainment
personalities, my cherub."*
"Is that like an actor or a clown, mama?"
"Yes, dear heart. It is. But without any of the talents."

The stern but kindly old umpire has called for stumps, the light is fading, the spectators drift away. But still the cricketing hero sits in the dressing rooms. Not for him the satisfied contemplation of a day well played, or the resolve to do better after a poor performance. For he stares into the future with blackness in his heart, the dread day has finally arrived: he is to retire from First Class Cricket.

Oh, unhappy hour! The moment he has despaired of for 15 years or more is here. Tomorrow he shall wake up, not with thoughts of a diligent session in the nets, or a game of cards with the fellows as the rain falls outside, or even assisting a friendly bookmaker with the correct course of a substantial wager on the current innings total, but with... nothing.

As he sits alone, at his lowest ebb, Old Stevens, the most beloved and decrepit of the pavilion attendants, knocks discreetly. A visitor is here.

Fig. 1. The Agent. More devious than a Frenchman.

An oily figure, he grasps the newly-retired player's hand too long to be sincere, his smile wolfish, his waistcoat too loud, suggestive of the stage or a petty criminal in Algiers. He is 'an agent' and he foresees a world of great opportunities for our hero. Would he like to hear them?

Performance in a 'ballroom dancing' competition. Making unfunny pleasantries with fellow retired sportsmen on the wireless radio. Being an advertising marionette for insurance companies and gambling operations.

Even, the most unkind offer of all, the modern transportation: to participate in the Australian jungle freakshow *I'm A Notable Personage... Please Assist Me In Extricating Myself From This Present Complicatedness*, forced to cavort alongside ageing actresses and disgraced vaudeville showmen in exchange for a few coins and the sickly sweet oxygen of public recognition.

Our cricketer recoils in horror, but these are the options open to the modern sportsman upon retirement, eking out an existence on the lowest rung of the entertainment ladder.

Either that, or coaching the likes of S.J. Mahmood and L.E. Plunkett to bowl straight.

Our hero wipes away a single unmanly tear.

Fig. 2. Product Endorsement. Like prostitution, but with better hours.

He shakes the agent's hand.

Tomorrow: the first engagement of his new life. A professional-amateur 'Charity Golf Day' in which he is to make up a foursome with the former Essex bat R.C. Irani, the music hall entertainer Mr James Tarbuck and the former heavyweight contender Mr Frank 'Big Frank' Bruno.

And he has only "got this gig", explains his new agent, "because Tuffers has double-booked with opening a grocery emporium in Hendon".

Oh Mother Cricket: how you give, and how you take away.

FOR THE LADY

COMPRISING: MATTERS THAT MAY BE OF INTEREST
TO THE FEMALE 'MIND'

Leg-Spin Marvel Offered To Show Me His Googly, Claims Nurse

Mr S.K. Warne is as famed for his *heart-breaks* as his leg-breaks, but this time the Australian spin bowler may have overstepped the *boundary* of gentlemanly conduct.

According to a nurse at the hair restoration clinic where Mr Warne occasionally undertakes promotional activity, a recent visit found the popular spinner less concerned with his *bowling figures* than the *figures* of the attendant female assistants.

One particular *maiden* to *bowl* Mr Warne *over* was a comely red-head by the name of Flora Pottage.

"I noticed that Mr Warne repeatedly threw glances in my direction," says Miss Pottage, a trained nurse who, to the eternal shame of her family, harbours ambitions of the stage.

"As he was preparing to leave after his treatment, I remarked that it was quite a warm day."

The shameless spinner replied: "Yes. Quite warm."

Mr Warne. Not his own hair.

"And then he left as if nothing had happened," confirms Miss Pottage. "Of course, I never saw him again, the bounder."

We are sure the estimable Mrs Warne will be overcome with interest at this tale of *tweakery* most saucy - and wonder if Mr Warne may well find himself on a *sticky wicket*!

Editor's Note: Rest assured, gentle lady reader, Miss Pottage has since been imprisoned for aggravated strumpetry.

Ask Uncle Cricket!

This issue, Uncle Cricket
shall be Seen and Not Heard,
an example you young fellows
should do very well to follow.

COMPETITION:

A CHILD MAY COLOUR-IN THIS ALLEGORICAL DEPICTION
OF ENGLAND'S GLORIOUS ASHES VICTORY AND SUBMIT HIS
EFFORTS TO THE EDITOR, WHEREUPON A WINNER SHALL
BE DECLARED. A BOTTLE OF PORT BEING 1ST PRIZE.

THE ACTING EDITOR'S JUDGEMENT SHALL BE FINAL.

Dr Grace's School for Cricket

Lesson Three: Bowling In A Manner Destined To Discombobulate The Batsman

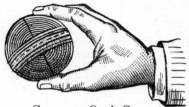

Changing One's Grip

For the Bowler rusé it is a simple matter to alter the flight and bounce of his delivery through small adjustments to the distribution of his fingers, the rigidity of his wrist and the stiffness of his upper lip.

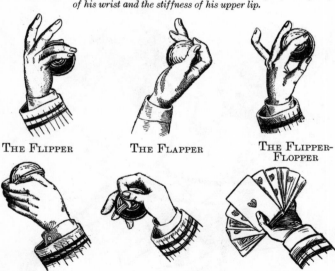

THE FLIPPER	THE FLAPPER	THE FLIPPER-FLOPPER
THE SNORTER	THE SNIFTER	THE PRESTIDIGITATOR

Evidently, when bowling to a Gentleman, as opposed to a Player, the intended nature of the delivery should be declared before the ball is bowled.

UNGENTLEMANLY LINES & DEVIANT PRACTICES
*No gentleman should dream to tamper with the ball, perhaps by raising the seam
with a nail, stopping it with his foot, roughening one side with a bottle fastener
or applying saliva mixed with Doctor Minty's Minty Fresh Mouth Sweet as he
shines. We list these methods so that you may avoid their replication.*

THE CORRIDOR OF UNCERTAINTY
Where S=Line of Off Stump; E=Elevation; W=Width of Batsman's Beard

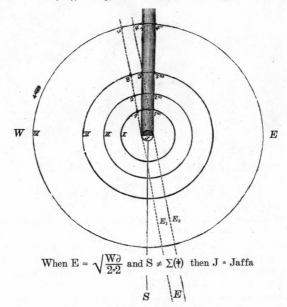

When $E \approx \sqrt{\dfrac{W\partial}{2 \cdot 2}}$ and $S \neq \Sigma(\dagger)$ then J = Jaffa

OPPORTUNITES FOR FURTHER STUDY
*No bowler's repertoire shall be complete without the inclusion of three further
deliveries, whose natures may best be learnt by close study of their originators.*

I. THE ONE THAT GOES AWAY
Mr G. McGrath, of Delhi

II. THE ONE THAT NEVER COMES BACK
Mr S. Harmison, of Durham

III. THE ONE AND ONLY
Mr Chesney Hawkes, of Slough Seconds

THE PAVILION OF HORRORS

THE THIRD INSTALMENT OF OUR VAMPIRIC SHOCKER...

We left Eliza in the gentlemen's dressing room at Lord's, staring in horror at the bloody corpse of her fellow scullery maid Peggy. The poor girl had evidently been devoured by a creature of the night, and now our heroine faces the same fate. Can she save herself and her one true love, the dashing batsman Johnny Brawnston-Smyth, from the vampires — and still get an acceptable seat from which to watch the opening exchanges of Yorkshire versus MCC?

"I'm going to enjoy eating you, Eliza Tanner, you scrawny little sneak," said Mrs Mordeth. She had some blood, which could only be Peggy's, down the front of her house-keeper's outfit. She leered.

"You are a vampire too?" gasped Eliza.

"Oh, there's plenty of us here at Lord's, my gal," sneered Mrs Mordeth, looming towards the terrified youngster like the un-compromising Australian pace bowler M.G. Hughes about to ask a tail-ender if he was born out of wedlock, or if he practised the ghastly sin of self-abuse and whether or not his dear mama was a fallen woman.

"We're everywhere, us vampires. Committee members, staff, players, the stewards. Especially the stewards."

"I knew there was something wrong with those miserable old sods," muttered Eliza.

"Oh yes, the St John's Wood headquarters of Cricket is teeming with the undead," said Mrs Mordeth. "And we'll all have a lovely snack on your juicy, hot young blood at about a four o'clock today, I shouldn't wonder."

Eliza thought quickly. There appeared no way out of the room, and she could surely not win a fight against Mrs Mordeth if the brute got hold of her. She must provoke the creature into a rage and strike swiftly.

"But you can't be a vampire," said Eliza. "You're too fat. I thought you were supposed to drink blood, not eat dripping and cakes. And aren't vampires supposed to be evil but beautiful? You're rough."

It had the desired effect. Mrs Mordeth roared in anger and lunged at Eliza, her fangs extended and a hideous hissing sound coming from her throat, a noise similar to that made by the more hidebound members when the possibility of allowing foreigners into the pavilion was raised at the last committee meeting.

Mrs Mordeth pounced, but Eliza grabbed a bat that was leaning up against the wall. The old trout flailed her burly arms, and Eliza leaped forward in the air, as she had seen Victor Trumper do in the newspaper photographs, and swung the bat very hard. It struck Mrs Mordeth a mighty crack on the knee. The vampiric below-stairs tyrant howled in pain and Eliza whirled the bat through the air, picturing dear, brave Johnny dispatching a long-hop through deep backward square. The bat whistled as it connected crisply with Mrs Mordeth's temple. Mrs Mordeth slumped on the floor, unconscious before she hit the ground. Eliza ran for the door, scrambled desperately with the key and was about to run as fast as she could down the stairs and away from there for ever.

But what about poor Johnny? How could she leave him to this hideous fate? She must now speak to him directly and take her chances even if it spelled her own doom. She hurried down to the Nursery Ground, praying that he would still be at the nets. Of course he was! Dear, diligent Johnny, carefully practising his 'tuck' - snapping the bat crisply under the arm so as to be able to walk off in a dignified manner if dismissed. Eliza sidled round the back of the net.

"Mr Brawnston-Smyth," she whispered. But he did not seem to hear. Her heart pounded with fear, and a little thrill at speaking to her hero for the first time. She tried again louder.

"Mr Brawnston-Smyth!"

"What's that? Hullo?" He turned around.

He looked startled and a little cross, but softened when he saw Eliza. She really was an awfully pretty girl, for a guttersnipe.

"Hello there, youngster," said Johnny. "Now what can I do for you?"

There seemed to be nothing for it but complete honesty.

"Mr Brawnston-Smyth," she said. "It's Miss Wellington. Your intended is a vampire, sir. So are the groundstaff, players and committee members. Even some of the amateurs, sir," she said.

"Good God," said Johnny. "Not the amateurs. Well I never. Gentlemen bloodsuckers, eh? How absolutely rum. Do you know, one of the fellows at Oxford was said to be a vampire, quite a useful left-armer and not a bad bat, especially on wet wickets, and he did have the most peculiar teeth. Now some of the chaps said he was a... you know... one of Nosferatu's lot, because he always wanted to stay on the paddock towards the close of play, even if the light was terrible, but then I rather fancied that was because he was a little shy about getting undressed after the match and hopping in the old bathtub with the fellows."

Eliza was not sure how much more of this upper-class twittery she could stand.

"Mr Brawnston-Smyth. Johnny. Listen to me, sir. Your fiancée is a blood-sucking fiend who wants to feed on your blood and trap you forever in a shadowy limbo between death and wakening, like a lost soul adrift on a sea of blood and pain, only with more County Cricket. Or that's what it said in this book, at least, sir."

It seemed to snap the affable but mentally feeble upper-crust batsman out of his reverie.

"Honoraria? A vampire?" said Johnny. "Well, I can't say I am surprised. She hardly eats at all, and she'll only ever come out and do anything when it's overcast. Totally hopeless on a sunny day."

"Like the Lancashire seamer Mr Anderson," ventured Eliza, shyly.

"That's right," laughed Johnny. "Or poor old Hoggy."

"After he lost his nip," giggled Eliza.

"Well, talking of nip, I must say there's nothing wrong with yours, young lady," said Johnny, with a raffish grin. "May I be permitted to know your name?"

Eliza blushed deeply, but smiled up at him nonetheless.

"It's Eliza, sir," she said.

"Well, Eliza. I suppose we ought to get going before we're turned into tea for a hungry vampire, eh what?"

He strode manfully down the net, tossed his gloves to the floor, walked up to Eliza and grabbed her firmly by the hand. Together they walked quickly towards the pavilion. Eliza felt scared, stunned, and deliriously happy. With Johnny by her side, surely anything was possible — even defeating an army of undead cricket enthusiasts!

To Be Continued...

COULD ROMANCE BLOSSOM BETWEEN THE SKIVVY AND THE STAR BATSMAN? WHAT CAN THEY DO ABOUT MISS WELLINGTON AND HER BLOODTHIRSTY COHORTS? IS MRS MORDETH DEAD? WHY IS THE IDIOTIC JOHNNY LEADING ELIZA TOWARDS, RATHER THAN AWAY FROM, MORTAL PERIL? ALL WILL BE REVEALED IN THE FINAL, CONCLUDING PART OF THE PAVILION OF HORRORS!

ALSO IN THE FORTHCOMING ISSUE!

Cricketer found in Nova Scotia: considerably alarming pictures... Rear Admiral D.P. Hornblower on Cricket as a disciplinary tool in The Navy... Isotonic opiates: the perfect antidote to pre-innings nerves... Could New Zealand be a Marxist plot?... Should the Derbyshire stalwart Mr Kim Barnett retire?... Donald Mattingwicket-Lawrence on the game in public schools: further considerably alarming pictures...

PROCURE ONE BY FAIR MEANS OR FOUL...

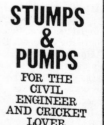
LITERATURE

EDITED BY MONTGOMERY
'INKY' PATTERSON

A most illuminating treat is in store for readers this month as we proudly present some verse from the finest poet in all Australia, Bongo Macgregor.

Mr Macgregor first rose to standing in Australian literary circles with his 1892 romantic epic *Jeez Blue, That Jumpbuck Looks Like A Sheila*. However, it was his collection *I'd Rather Have A Tuckerbag Than A Pommie At Second Slip* (1895), a synthesis of federalist sentiment and unfettered disgust at the standard of catching in the 1894–1895 Ashes series, that propelled Mr Macgregor into the first rank of poets.

We are immeasurably honoured to present a poem from his forthcoming collection, *A Swagman In The Bottle-O*.

I Can See The Pub From Here

by bongo macgregor

Aussie! Aussie! Aussie! Oi! Oi! Oi!
Cried the blokes as they played at a variety of manly sports
with awesome competitiveness
Dirty, hot, hard and unyielding
And that was just the players.

Jeez it was a warm one
Out there in Woolongobba Gorge
15 required and the last pair together
Good manly fellows enjoying a roll in the sheepdip

And along came Pommie, with his red coats and his guns
and his superior attitude
Shot all the boys down in cold blood
"Aw mate," said the dying lads. "At least let us finish
our tinnies first."
But Pommie he just laughed, and awarded himself a dodgy
leg before, and a cigar

But as they bled their last in the red Woolongobba earth
Old Bill spoke up, with his final breath
"Never mind about Pommie, you blokes," he said.
"I reckon I can see the pub from here."

IN HONOUR OF THE ASHES SERIES THAT IS OUR FOCUS
THIS EDITION, MRS CECILY BEASTING IS DELIGHTED
TO WELCOME THE AUSTRALIAN AGONY AUNT
MRS MADGE BISHOP TO ANSWER READERS' QUESTIONS

Mesdames Beasting & Bishop,
  Is it correct practice to clap an opposing bowler should he be fielding in front of one's position in the grandstand?
  —Mrs Titty Bresnan, Yorkshire

Mrs Beasting writes: Absolutely this is the correct way to behave. All opponents should be treated with courtesy. However, if the opposing bowler has the rank of Baronet or higher (or an Archdeacon, if a 'man of the cloth', or a full Colonel in The Army), then he should only be addressed indirectly, out of deference to his standing.

. . .

Mrs Bishop writes: Bugger that for a laugh, just chuck a bottle at his head, the mongrel. If you can slash in it first, go for your life. I once bagged the Essex no-mark D.R. Pringle full in his fat head with a can-full of gypsy's on the third man boundary at Melbourne in the summer of 1889-1890. Ripper!

Mesdames Beasting & Bishop,
  What is the correct picnic to pack for a day at the Cricket with my aged mother-in-law, nephews and an unmarried female acquaintance?
  —Mrs P.T. Bowen, Lancaster

Mrs Beasting writes: This does indeed require some preparation due to the differing tastes of the generations, etc. - and their propensity for making a mess! I should suggest a small plucked fowl or potted kidney for your mother-in-law, a cold collation for the unmarried lady and some form of sticky cake for the little ones.

• • •

Mrs Bishop writes: Beer. For yourself, to take the edge off a day with the old bat. For her, beer, so she'll hopefully drop off and give you a bit of peace and flaming quiet. Ditto the kiddies: beer for the same reason. The unmarried wossername sounds like a rug-muncher to me, so she'll be right with a cold one, but careful she doesn't get pickled and try to have a rummage in your dung-hampers down at the Nursery End bogs. Cheers.

 # PERSONAL NOTICES

MCGRATH'S Metronomes: Improve your Accuracy and learn to 'sledge' in perfect syncopation.

BATSMAN seeks large pie. Must not lead to weight gain. Please contact Samit Patel via pavilion at Trent Bridge or behind The Old Bakery, High Street, Nottingham most mornings. No gentlemen of the press or England selectors.

COME SEE Mr Gavin Hamilton, the amazing cricketing Scotchman, perform feats of hitting, clean bowling and catching of the cricket ball - *all of which he undertakes without recourse to alcoholic drink.* This non-drunken Scotch cricketer is truly the marvel of the age and a treat for all the family. Barnet Fair, Barnet, Sunday.

MR JASON GILLESPIE, the noted Australian fast man, is available for frightening children at parties, school fetes, prize-giv-ings etc. Mr Gillespie has a bicycle for transport and his nose is his own. Apply: The Australian High Commission, c/o The Cat And Bastard Pub, Shepherd's Bush

---

WILHELMINA. How I yearn for your 'ring saving one'. May I call upon you? W

NAVVIES! Learn to swear like an Australian debutante. PO Box 196, London.

FOUND, at Old Trafford Cricket ground during Test match: small Australian left-hander, good worker, can field at slip or in covers. Would suit County side or travelling circus. Answers to name of Alfie. Two guineas or best offer.

THE HOME FOR FALLEN WOMEN CRICKETERS
Box 132
Truro

FACTS ABOUT
THE EXCITING
AUSTRALIAN
FAST MAN
M.G. JOHNSON

Mitchell Johnson's Christian name is unique in his family: every other male Johnson has the given names 'Plugger Alf', as do several of the females.

Mitchell Johnson regards W.G. Grace as the most trustworthy bearded man he has ever met, with the exception of his close friend Dr Sigmund Freud.

Mitchell Johnson can play the bassoon, although he finds it upsetting to do so.

Mitchell Johnson is afraid of: needles, spiders, the dark, doors that are left open, doors that are shut, economics, the collected works of Lord Byron, being hit over the head with the collected works of Lord Byron, a nagging sense of cosmic meaningless, off-spinners and the letter 'F'.

Mitchell Johnson is famed in the Australian team for his pleasant manner. Only once has he blotted his copybook, when a bridge game with the New Zealand ambassador descended into acrimony and Mitchell Johnson bit His Excellency's wife on the arm.

Mitchell Johnson so enjoyed Australia's 1893 tour of America that he considered abandoning Cricket altogether to become a rodeo clown.

Mitchell Johnson reportedly inspired Bram Stoker to write Dracula, specifically the hideous gurgling noise that the Australian paceman makes while eating a Bath Oliver.

Mitchell Johnson socialises regularly with the operatic librettist, Mr William Gilbert, and suggested the plot of *The Mikado* to him after the pair enjoyed an amusing round of golf together at Royal Troon. Mr Arthur Sullivan is acutely jealous of Mitchell Johnson and will brook no mention of the Australian's name in his presence.

A 24-Hour Period In The Daily Existence Of...

Fat Freddie Flintstone

BEING A MOST INSIGHTFUL WINDOW INTO THE ACTIVITIES
AND HABITS OF THE POPULAR ALL-ROUND SPORTSMAN AND
SCOURGE OF THE TEMPERANCE MOVEMENT

ELEVEN O'CLOCK...

I awake in, or at least near to, the bed. I fancy I feel something peculiar on my face. I examine myself in the looking glass and see that some rapscallion has written 'twat' upon it — this being some species of Greek or Latinate jest, I presume. I soundly thrash my man, Harmison, as a punishment, for two hours.

ONE O'CLOCK...

I fear that this strenuous activity has aggravated some part of my injured personage, so I have a short rest and fill a bath with ice. After the application of some barrels of gin, I have fashioned a primitive but refreshing concoction. I shall call it 'A Bath Full Of Gin'.

SEVEN O'CLOCK...

To a function with my business manager and factotum, Mr C.G. 'Pongo' Codrington. From what I can divine, the reception is to advertise a new brand of cricket bat, or possibly a syrupy mixture giving of energy and vitality to the imbiber.

TEN O'CLOCK...

I appear in a music hall act entitled *A League Of Their Own* wherein a fat man poses questions about the sports of football (both codes), Cricket and badger-baiting and occasionally offers amusing barbs about myself and other sportsmen. People seem to enjoy it; I myself do not. I instruct Harmison to bring a hansom cab to the stage door and we exit swiftly to the nearest brewery.

THREE O'CLOCK...

Turn in early as have important cricket match tomorrow.

Witness First-Hand One Of The World's Most Thrilling Sights:

GATTING'S PASSAGE

SEE THE ASHES IN AUSTRALIA WITH SOME OF THE GAME'S FINEST FORMER LEGENDS

Featuring, but not limited to:

A Champagne Breakfast
(Note: Champagne extra) (Additional note: Breakfast extra)

Drinks Reception with the imperious former Leicestershire bat Mr D.I. Gower (note: Mr Gower will not address tour party directly, nor be present at actual drinks reception)

A chance to be sworn at quite roughly by Mr John Emburey

An opportunity to purchase match tickets at a grossly inflated price

Repatriation in event of death (coffin extra)

All your medical inoculations performed upon you by a County professional of your choosing

RETURN TICKETS AVAILABLE

Steamship shown is for illustrative purposes only. Actual vessel may not be strictly seaworthy. Terms & Conditions apply.

Winter 1896
— The Future Of Cricket —

THE
WISDEN
CRICKETER

Vol. I - No 4   WINTER 1896   PRICE ONE PENNY

In memoriam: Roderick Jarndyce, formerly Acting Editor of this magazine

The loss of Mr Jarndyce is a bitter blow. That a fine journalist should have been killed by falling masonry is a tragedy. And that the ghastly accident, for it was very much an accident, should happen underneath the very window of his publisher and dear friend, i.e. myself... Well, it is almost too much to bear. I shall never forgive myself for balancing that large ornamental rock upon the sill, nor attempting to secure it with an anvil and an upright pianoforte as counterweights.

Yet let us not dwell on the past, glorious though Mr Jarndyce's brief time at the helm may have been, for *The Wisden Cricketer* and the sport of Cricket are setting sail for the future. In this, our final issue of the year, we look forward and wonder what the greatest game may be like in ten, fifty, a hundred years' time and more.

Will it be played on Earth, or on other planets as well? Will wondrous technology have replaced the humble bat and ball with some devilish mechanical implements? Will Test matches take place underwater? Could a woman even learn to play the game?

As we can see illustrated by my last suggestion, the temptation to dream up entirely fanciful scenarios is a great one. However, we are most fortunate to have some of the wisest heads in Cricket and beyond to guide us through the exciting future.

On a personal level, I wish to thank all the staff at the magazine for supporting me fully in my new editorship, and especially the widow of poor Mr Jarndyce, Kitty, who has been of enormous personal comfort to me during this upsetting time.

—Mr Augustus Possett,
Publisher and Editor-in-Chief

CORRESPONDENCE:
AN OPPORTUNITY FOR READERS TO HAVE THEIR SAY UPON CRICKET, SOCIETY AND THE CONTENT OR PRODUCTION OF THIS PUBLICATION, NO MATTER HOW ILL-INFORMED THEIR VIEWS MAY BE

SIR, I am sure that many of your other readers have enjoyed the exertions of the former Yorkshire fast bowler Mr D. Gough on the popular vaudeville tour *Strictly Come Dancing*. Yet how can it be fair or just that men are allowed to vote for their favourite performer, while we women are not? I have written a letter to Mr Gough, and also to the ensemble's impresario Mr Len Goodman, and if I do not receive a reply I shall hurl myself under Mr Gough the next time I see him attempting the bolero.

 −*Emmeline Pankhurst (Mrs)*,
 HMP Holloway

SIR, All this talk of investigation into 'match fixing' is depressing and alarming. As a professional gambler, I have personally arranged for no fewer than seven closely contested County matches to be carefully 'thrown' in the last overs this season. I do not do this solely for my own pecuniary advantage, but also to ensure that an exciting time is had by all right up until the close of play. What would the paying public rather watch: a dull draw in which nobody makes any money just to keep the moaning moral minnies happy, or a thrilling stitch-up which ends in high drama and everyone with a few pennies in their pocket?

 −*G.W. Crooke*,
 East Ham

SIR, The sight of W.G. 'consoling' his vanquished Australian opponent (*TWC*, Autumn Issue) was neither inspiring nor noble, as your periodical contended. It was vile. Dr Grace had defeated the fellow fair and square, and should have finished him off with a cutlass, or at the very least, a billy club. After defeating Napoleon, did Wellington invite him round for tea or enquire as to the health of Josephine? Of course not. He locked the man up on an island in the middle of nowhere where he could not get into any more mischief: a state of affairs with which the Australian is historically familiar, and one that he could surely respect and understand, if not enjoy.

 −*Mr G.O.P. Sickert*
 Camden Town

BARMY ARMY INVADES PRUSSIA

AMBASSADOR RECALLED; SIX BEACH TOWELS RECOVERED

Johnny Foreigner was out for a duck last weekend when the mass ranks of the Barmington Army descended upon Prussia and routed Fritz on his home patch.

The sporting arenas and watering holes of the once-mighty European power proved quite unable to handle the sheer thirst of the Barmington Army in full flow.

And the native inhabitants found themselves stumped by the incessant singing, atonal trumpet voluntary and unsightly exposed flesh of the invaders.

After successful campaigns in Wales, the Low Countries and the Balearic Isles last summer, the Barmington Army's triumph was another stunning success for their leader Mr Jedediah 'Gutbuster' Giddins.

General Giddins led his best men, the Light Ale Brigade, in what looked a suicidal charge towards a crowded public bar

"C'est magnifique"

Fig. 1. 'Into The Valley Of Meths Rode The 600'

at the Von Liegbefürvikkett Stadium, the spiritual home of Prussian Cricket.

PANTALOONIES

Heroic defeat seemed the only possible outcome as the tiny band of obese English heroes, clad in nothing but Flag of St George short pantaloons and pith sun-hats, waddled determinedly towards the massed beer pumps.

Poignant indeed was the sound and spectacle as the Barmington Army marching band bugler-in-chief, Ebenezer Catchweasel, played a mournful *The Great Escape*.

So powerful was the sight of the few dozen overweight

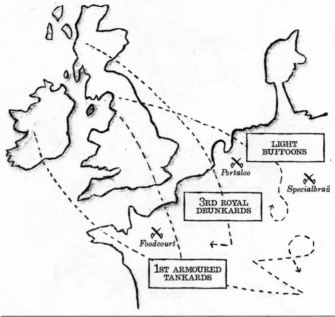

Fig. 2. The 1896 Campaign For Real Ale

Englishmen downing quart after quart of light ale, one French military observer was overheard to murmur: "C'est magnifique, mais ce n'est pas la bière."

PRUSSED OFF

However, within little more than 90 minutes of valiant alcoholic abuse, the entire bar had been drunk dry and all the Prussians had gone to sit somewhere else, muttering darkly about: "incessant noise" and "some most unamusing witticisms directed at the hosts".

The victorious men of the Barmington Army were then led in their regimental song of triumph, *There Were 99 Green Bottles...,* until they all fell asleep in the late afternoon and got sunburned.

All hail the heroically drunken ambassador-warriors of English Cricket!

Matters of Lesser or Negligible Interest:

ALARMING developments in the British Indian Empire, where Maharajah Lalit Modi has become far too big for his sandals. Obsessed by his own cleverness and the self-styled success of his Indian Pre-Eminent League sideshow, he now proposes a 'Player Auction'. Are our finest cricketing talents to fall into the grip of the white slave trade? Action must and will be taken.

A MOST enjoyable and informative séance was held at the Old Town Hall, Mary-le-bone on the last day of October. Several cricketing personages of import were present to behold the efforts spiritual of the famous medium, Gypsy Rose Trescothick. After a period hiding in a cupboard shrieking, Madame Trescothick was lured out with sausage meat, and was soon successful in contacting a spirit answering to the name of Bouffant Bill. This spectre claimed that it had previously been the hairdresser of several prominent cricketers, including: Mr Brett Lee of Australia, Mr Ryan Sidebottom of Nottinghamshire and Mr Brian Close of Yorkshire, although the last-named cricketer may have been a piece of deliberate misinformation upon the part of the ghostly crimper.

THE POPULAR spin bowler G.P. Swann has lost his beloved pet cat, Tweet, possibly after driving his recently purchased 'motorised automobile' while drunk and forgetting where he had left the creature.

THE CRICKETING suffragette Rachel Tally-Ho Flint will be at The Surrey Oval on November 14th to give a lecture about the role of women in the game, and to burn down the pavilion.

Mr E.T. SMITH of Cambridge University, Middlesex and Kent has written another of his celebrated books. It is not recommended to the mentally enfeebled or those who prefer their sportsmen to be of the uncomplicated type of personality.

For One Night ONLY

THE BALL OF THE CENTURY

Leg-Break Ballroom
Shane Street, Trafford

DEBUTANTES WELCOME

Men Of Planet Earth Versus Creatures From The Planet Mars

A thrilling contest was played out in the rarefied atmosphere of the Mars Cricket Stadium as Earth won back the Interplanetary Ashes 3-2 after defeating the Martians by two space wickets.

Remarkable advances in efficiency of course mean that only six players are needed per side, but the Martian hosts required but four of their batsmartians in posting a commanding total of 998-2 declared. Their multi-tentacled opener Zob was particularly impressive, playing shots all around the wicket on his way to a superb unbeaten 365, aided no doubt by having six limbs with which to wield the bat.

Some of the Earth bowlers found it hard going in the oxygen-free conditions, but toiled humanfully to restrict their hosts on a lifeless, red pitch. The ground control of Major Tom was instrumental in giving the well-travelled left armer a brace of Martian scalps.

However, it was the cryogenically frozen colossus, C.B. Fry, who was the real hero for the Men of Earth, the veteran Sussex man blasting his way to

Fig. 1. Mr C.B. Fry

an astonishing 678 space runs in reply, despite having no corporeal body and being just a ghastly head in a bell jar.

There was an unfortunate incident when the Mechanised Umpiring Machine malfunctioned and attacked the Mars opening bowler after a contentious LBW appeal. A nasty interplanetary War of the Worlds was only averted by the diplomatic intervention of Ranji's great-great grandson, Anji and the whole Earth (i.e. British Empire) celebrated an unlikely victory.

The Martians will be on Earth for the return fixture next year, ahead of an eagerly anticipated triangular series with the Venusians.

Men of Earth v Creatures of Mars
Played at Mars Cricket Stadium, June 4th 1986

Creatures From The Planet Mars VI

ZZ Zob	not out	365
PT Znark	b Major Tom	259
EF Znark *	c Grace b Major Tom	205
JJ Zerk *	not out	150
GW Zappity †	DNB	
JW Wilson	DNB	
Extras (space wides 6, nb 13) ...	....	19
Total	(for two declared)	998

Men Of Earth VI

CB Fry (frozen head thereof) *	not out	678
Anji	c Zob b Zerk	106
WG Grace Jr Jr Jr Jr	c Zerk b Zob	83
HG Wells	retired hurt	2
Major Tom	st Zappity b Znark	99
Dr S Cavor †	not out	3
Extras (sw 16, nb 12)	....	28
Total	(for four)	999

Note: H.G. Wells was obliged to retire after being struck by a flying time machine.

Dr Pontius Ponting's Patent

Mental Disintegrator

For Efficacious Removal Of Unwanted Batsmen From The Crease; Leaves No Trace Or Stain Of Character; May Be Safely Operated At Arm's Length Or Short Leg

'THE NITWITTER'

Bresnan, T., of Yorkshire and England Receives
a Missive from the Marvellous and Most Novel
Twittering Conversational Device, the Use
Thereof Which is Sweeping the Nation and her
Cricketers in Particular

A FLEETING INTERLOCUTION WITH MR P. 'DIDDY' COLLINGWOOD

A HEART-RENDING DEPICTION OF LIFE IN THE NORTH

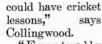

Your *Wisden Cricketer* asks Collingwood how he came to Cricket.

"When I was a young lad," says the weather-beaten, honest fellow. "Unlike certain other England captains I will not mention, I never had the benefit of coaching at one of the great public schools.

"Or any sort of school, in fact. We were too poor for that. We learned our sport the hard way, being beaten around the head and chest with a cricket bat on the freezing Northern tundra, and left out there to die if we could not stand it.

"That was up until the age of three-and-a half. Then something happened as changed my cricketing life."

Collingwood's mother took a fifth job, working as a bare-knuckle boxer. The few extra pennies would be spent on cricketing lessons for her youngest, who was showing promise as a fieldsman at point.

"Mother beat up all-comers, morning, noon and night so I could have cricket lessons," says Collingwood.

"Eventually we had enough money together so I could start a correspondence course. I was overjoyed."

But this proved to be a false dawn.

"The correspondence course was a disgrace," said Collingwood. "They would send you a ball in the post, and you would hit it.

"It was a tough education, and sometimes quite a boring one, because the balls only arrived every three months or so.

"But it made me value time at the crease, I can assure you, and I have never looked back since."

And there is a heart-warming end to this tale of perseverance in the face of hardship and the slowness of the postal service.

"Since I have been a player for England," beams Collingwood, "I now am paid enough money so as mam only has to take fights with middleweights or below, which is a great relief to all of us, particularly mam."

THE WONDERFUL & MYSTERIOUS WORLD WHICH SURROUNDS US

PUNDITOPOLY

BEING A STUDY OF THE EXCITING NEW TECHNIQUE OF 'COMMENTARY' BY WHICH SPECTATORS MAY BE APPRAISED OF EVENTS THEY HAVE HITHERTO WITNESSED ONLY WITH THEIR OWN EYES

In our last edition we learned a little about the barren wasteland that is the retired professional's life after Cricket. But help may be at hand! Thanks to the marvellous advances in technological cleverness, employment may be available for countless former cricketers in the new discipline of Cricket Commentary.

Leading the charge are the men of Mr Murdoch's *Sky-High Sports*, who are enlivening the Cricket viewing experience thanks to their so-called Commentary Blimp. On Test match days, former heroes including I.T. Botham, D.I. Gower and Dr D. Lloyd are to be found perched atop a splendid Navigable Balloon, soaring many hundreds of feet above the field of play and providing them unparalleled viewpoints with which to perfect their 'commentary' of the action unfolding below.

For the uninitiated, the practice of commentary consists of former Cricket greats describing the play and passing comment upon it, specifically with the purpose of implying — or, in the case of Botham, boldly stating — that things were a great deal better in their day and that they do not know what is going on out there.

Fig. 1. Commentary demands prodigious quantities of Hot Air

Fig. 2. The Art of 'Commentary'

This exciting communicative art is then relayed to the people on the surface of the Earth and provides those not fortunate enough to be present at a match an opportunity to keep abreast of the key passages of play.

Several methods of conveying the commentary are in development, including but not limited to: bellowing very loudly out of the side of the dirigible balloon; shouting the commentary down a large pipe;

writing the commentary down for the purpose of sending it via pigeon; and throwing less prestigious members of the commentary team (e.g. the affable former Warwickshire bat N.V. Knight) out of the balloon so he can pass on a message.

Fig. 4. Mr Botham makes his way home after the match

Fig. 3. Mr Knight prepares to relay events to the crowd below

The last-named proved most popular among commentators and spectators alike when pioneered at Trent Bridge recently, although the injuries sustained by Knight make this an impractical technique in the longer term.

Soon, without question, a marvellous invention will appear on the horizon to ensure that the thrilling commentary can be enjoyed by every Cricket-loving man, woman and child in England (or at least those well-off enough to pay a subscription for the service).

Fig. 5.
Mr I.D. Blackwell of Durham.
Not a balloon.

HOW A TYPICAL EXAMPLE OF 'COMMENTARY' MIGHT BE EXPECTED TO UNFOLD IN THE FUTURE

A summer afternoon at Lord's. The commentary balloon hovers majestically as men, women and alien visitors from the planet Neptune enjoy a splendid day's sport. The batsman has just struck a crisp drive through the covers.

MR GOWER:
Oh look, the batsman has just struck a crisp drive through the covers.

DR LLOYD:
Ecky thump! Bless my britches! Echo And T'Bunnymen!

MR KNIGHT:
Oooh, I just don't know, ooh, that's what I like to call a crisp drive, but on the other hand, you just feel, is it through the covers?

MR BOTHAM:
What a pathetic Jessie. I should have hit that three times as hard, and I should not have been whining while I was doing it, let me tell you.

MR WILLIS:
Heads will have to roll after that delivery, and no mistake.

THE COMMENTARY 'VIEWER' OR LISTENER:
Stick the wireless on, Mother.

A PROFOUND PROGNOSTICATION:

WHAT WILL CRICKET BE LIKE IN THE FUTURE?

THE WISDEN CRICKETER INVITES A PANEL OF EXPERT
PERSONS TO DISCUSS WHAT MAY LIE IN STORE FOR
CRICKET IN THE NEXT CENTURY AND BEYOND

OUR PONTIFICATORS:

DR W.G. GRACE
CRICKETING NONPAREIL
AND OWNER OF THE FINEST
BEARD IN ENGLAND

MR ALEISTER CROWLEY
PROMISING YOUNG
OCCULTIST, OFF-SPINNER
AND ALCHEMIST WHO
HOPES ONE DAY TO BE THE
WICKEDEST MAN IN
THE WORLD

FLORENCE NIGHTINGALE
LADY WITH THE LAMP,
NATIONAL HEROINE
AND ACCOMPLISHED
WICKETKEEPER-BAT

DR CECIL RHODES
POTENTATE, RECENTLY
RETIRED PRIME MINISTER
OF THE CAPE COLONY
AND IMPORTER-EXPORTER
OF FRUIT, DIAMONDS AND
CRICKETERS

JULES VERNE
UNDERWATER FRENCHMAN

Dr Grace: I expect there to be significant attention paid to the development of an Umpire Review System. In my long years playing the game, I have yet to meet an umpire who was not either a fool or a knave, and the sooner we batsmen can start telling the fellows exactly what is what, the better. Why should a day's entertainment be ruined just because some uppity little functionary falsely believes me to have edged behind? I should like to see all contentious decisions reviewed by an expert committee, i.e. me, with stiff penalties for umpires who show dissent, perhaps flogging or prison for repeated offenders.

Dr Rhodes: The teams of the Cape will be overrun with cricketers from England seeking a better life there.

Miss Nightingale: It pains me to say it, but I fear the Indian may have some considerable influence in how the game is administered.

Monsieur Verne: Technological advances will mean that your sport of Cricket will be played on The Moon, on giant hovering pitches in the sky, and under the bed of the deepest oceans. And while you English nancy boys are doing this, I shall be defiling your womenfolk with my giant Octopus Propelled Submarine and inventing new ways to be unkind to geese.

Mr Crowley: Indeed, I too have seen this in my experiments with opiates and cricketing statistics from back editions of *Wisden*. And in my travellings of the mind and the blackness of my soul, I saw a great beast of the Golden Dawn, and the number of the beast was 666, which incidentally will be the number of runs scored by Derbyshire after tea on the final day to win the County Championship at Headingley in September 1975.

The panel was dissolved after Miss Nightingale struck Monsieur Verne around the head with her Lamp, although it should be put on record that she did furnish the bloodied Gallic fantasist with a bandage afterwards.

THE CRICKETER OF THE FUTURE

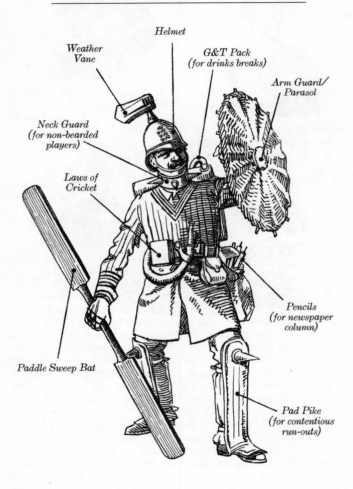

Helmet

Weather
Vane

G&T Pack
(for drinks breaks)

Arm Guard/
Parasol

Neck Guard
(for non-bearded
players)

Laws of
Cricket

Pencils
(for newspaper
column)

Paddle Sweep Bat

Pad Pike
(for contentious
run-outs)

The Umpire Of The Future

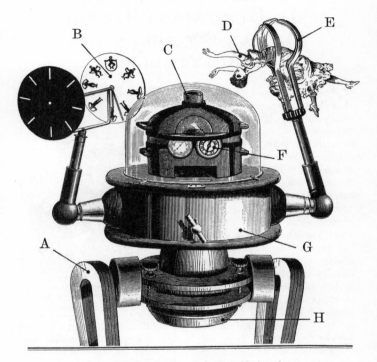

A – Polished steel carapace for intimidating glare
B – Kinetoscopic Action Re-Imaginator to allow repeated
contemplation of contentious passages of play
C – Head
D – Lady Cricketer
E – Lady Cricketer Eradicator
F – Tea Interval Chronometer
G – Hat storage unit for caps, jerseys and other clothing
H – Codpiece

A MOST PERSONAL PROBING

MR DUCKWORTH-LEWIS: A MAN OF FORESIGHT AND INTELLECT

Everywhere we look in England today, men of great cleverness are inventing ways to make our lives safer, healthier, more rewarding (with the exception of the lower orders) and above all else, more efficient. From the marvellous motorised machines currently terrorising our roads, to disgusting instant photographic pictures of indiscreetly attired ladies, and from the vast sewing machines that enable humble-born girls the dignity of labouring 19 hours a day making hatpins, to the steam-powered venereal cures patented by Dr P.P. Cocrotte, we truly live in an age of both wonder and speed.

Cricket is not lagging behind - and this is in no small part due to the splendid work of that most inspired of mathematical bamboozlers, Mr Reginald Duckworth-Lewis. Mr Duckworth-Lewis is a man of verve, vim and vision, and here relays his own contribution to the march of progress.

"It started two seasons ago, when I was at The Oval, at

Fig. 1. Mr Duckworth-Lewis. Bit of an Egghead.

about four o'clock on the final day of a quite engrossing contest between Surrey and Middlesex," recalls Duckworth-Lewis. "Now, Middlesex needed to make about 85 in 32 overs, but Lohmann and Richardson were on their mettle and matters could scarcely have been more delicately poised.

"Most irritatingly, I had to leave the ground in order to catch a train to a family engagement, and I was forced to depart before I could see the dénouement."

The top-rate scientist is seldom more dangerous than when he is vexed by a problem, or under the influence of powerful narcotics, and Duckworth-Lewis vowed that he should never again be forced by circumstance to miss the end of an exciting match.

"It struck me that, rather than go through the time-consuming business of playing all these cricket matches, I might be able to fashion a machine that would compute their correct outcomes, thus saving a good deal of time and bother," he says.

He began work immediately on The Duckworth-Lewis Cricketing Outcome Predictor Difference Engine.

It was an inspired mechanical creation, fashioned of valves and with a powerful mercury-powered motor which exploded repeatedly during testing, covering Duckworth-Lewis with the toxic loopy juice on more than one occasion. He 'taught' the machine the Laws of the game and over 10,000 examples of previous match outcomes, factoring in such matters as strength of batting and bowling attacks, weather, state of the game, size of crowd and corruptibility of umpires and participants.

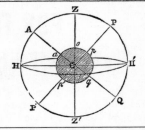

Fig. 2. Some Science.

"The results were, if I say so myself, quite eerily accurate," declares Duckworth-Lewis. "For instance, only last month I instructed the machine to predict the result of a two-innings match between an MCC All-England XI and Great Missenden Infant School for Girls' Team at the Melbourne Cricket Ground. The Predictor Difference Engine was of the opinion that the Great Missenden team would most likely triumph by an innings and perhaps 75 or 80 runs.

"Those girls can be very hard to bowl at on a flat pitch," he explained. "I wrote a letter to MCC informing them of their XI's defeat and asking them to send a cheque in recompense for my predictive work, but as yet there has been no reply."

Is Duckworth-Lewis condemned to be a visionary before his time, or will his brilliant methods one day be deciding imaginary cricket matches the globe over? We fervently hope the latter...

FOR THE LADY

The Flighty, Feisty, Fantastical CRABs

In the Golden Age of the 1860s, the Lady Cricket enthusiast may well have fanned herself vigorously at the sight of a dashing young bowler shining the ball against his creamy pantaloons, but she was sure to keep a safe and modest distance from the sportsman, who was likely to be either voraciously uncouth, poor, or both.

However, with cricketers becoming richer, and young women becoming more wanton, some modern females are going so far as to invite romantic attention from the heroes of the game. With their eye-catching fashions, willingness to be photographed in the popular press and outrageous absence of decorum, these CRABs (Companions Romantic and Betrothed) have become almost as celebrated as their Cricket-playing menfolk.

Of late, there have been rumblings of disapproval that the CRABs may prove a distraction to the England XI from the important business of playing in Australia this winter. Some have suggested that the CRABs should not be allowed to travel, while others advocate that they be sent to prison for diverting

Fig. 1. A CRAB at sea

men of England from their Cricket. After careful consideration, this publication adjudges that latter course of action to be harsh, and instead recommends the CRABs be permitted to travel to Australia *providing they are given berths on a separate tramp steamer to the men.*

This seems the fairest solution, and the one that will encourage the least amount of cabin-fevered tomfoolery on the long passage over.

Ask Uncle Cricket!

The Question Of The Reverse Sweep

The 1875 Act of Parliament outlawing the use of the Sweep is among the most injurious and harmful pieces of legislation of our time.

In the opinion of Uncle Cricket, the Sweep is a most effective technique and all of you youngsters are well advised to acquaint yourselves with it.

Thus you can achieve some usefulness on the pitch and off it, no matter how lowly your station in life.

I urge all right-thinking young urchins to aid the circumvention of this shameful mollycoddling and offer themselves up to their domestic employers for use in what might be termed 'The Reverse Sweep'.

Fig. 1.
The sadly prohibited practice

Fig. 2.
"I loves being a Reverse Sweep, if it please you, ma'am"

NOTES:

DR GRACE'S SCHOOL FOR CRICKET

LESSON FOUR:
NOVEL CRICKET SHOTS OF THE FUTURE.
COMPILED BY GUEST LECTURER MR K.P. PIETERSEN

THE BOOYAKASHA-KAZAAM
Double-bladed Shaolin Kick with half-pike.
A tariff of 6.3, rising to 6.9 when deployed on horseback.

THE STENA LINE STAB
Eyepatch optional.

THE RHINOPLASTIFICATOR
Bowl me a bouncer. Go on, I dare you.

THE PAVILION OF HORRORS

THE FINAL INSTALMENT IN OUR SERIAL...

We left Eliza and Johnny inexplicably striding towards confron-
tation with the evil vampires of Lord's - can their love survive a
furious assault by a fired-up undead attack? Or will their very
souls be devoured before close of play in The Pavilion Of Horrors?

Eliza walked with Johnny across the Nursery Ground as if in a trance. How could he have borne so phlegmatically the shocking revelation that his fiancée was a vampire? Was his nature simply as fearless as his batting? Or was it because he had the intellectual capacity of a potato? With her slender hand in his manly mitt, she scarcely cared.

They must defeat the vampires by the time Yorkshire arrived in the morning - the great Northern county's at-titude towards supernatural personages of non-Yorkshire extraction being frosty in the extreme. The men from Headingley had already this season threatened to boycott a match against Gloucestershire after a rumour sprang up that the men of the South West numbered a Welshman and a warlock in their XI. Fortunately it had proven untrue, at least about the Welshman, and a serious incident was averted. But who knew what scandal could envelop MCC if the men from Headingley had to share a playing area with people not only born outside of Yorkshire - but born outside of the human race!

It was clear to Eliza that the very future of Cricket depended upon their vanquishing the vampires without fuss or alarm. She was just about to ask Johnny what they should do when he spoke.

"You know," began Johnny. "Well... the thing is... Eliza."

"Yes?" she said.

"Well... the thing is, I have always noticed you here, you know. At Lord's, I mean. You know, going about your work. I must say, you are frightfully lovely."

Eliza's heart soared through the air, like a used beer pot thrown from the balcony at Melbourne onto the head of an English seam bowler grazing at long leg.

"Do you really think so?" she said.

"Oh yes," said Johnny. "I may be as thick as W.G. Grace's beard, but I know a delightful filly when I see one."

"But I am but a humble scullery maid, sir," said Eliza. "And you are the finest gentleman cricketer in all of England."

"I don't care for any of that, Eliza," said Johnny. "I love you. I have always loved you. As much as I loved scoring 103

not out against Surrey at The Oval when I knew I had gloved one behind when I was on two. As much as I love putting on my left pad before my right. As much as I love listening to Sir Geoffrey talk about the time up at Scarb—"

"Yes, yes, dear heart," said Eliza. "Do get on with it. It's like Jam Sahib Dravid's epic 12 at the Kensington Oval over here."

"Absolutely," said Johnny. "Well, here's the thing. Come away with me, Eliza. Let us run away to The Cape, or Australia, or Somerset or one of those other far away places, and I will earn us a living by playing Cricket, and in the evenings, we will oil our bats and talk about the averages of the great bowlers and who would get in our all-time Hampshire XI."

"Oh Johnny!" said Eliza.

"Oh Eliza!" said Johnny.

"Oh Johnny!" said Eliza.

"Oh Eliza!" said Johnny, as he took her in his arms and kissed her.

"Oh, Jesus Christ, pass the sick bag," hissed a female voice.

Eliza froze. So did Johnny.

Mrs Mordeth, sporting a livid black eye, glared at her. Alongside her stood Miss Wellington, smoking a long cigarette with one hand and torturing a Pekinese with the other.

"Well, well," said Miss Wellington. "The batsman and the skivvy. Oh, Johnny. I thought you knew better than to attempt to score out of the rough."

Her eyes locked on to Johnny's and a distressing change came over him almost at once. He seemed to shrink visibly, bent to Miss Wellington's will as she stared coldly into his heart.

"Absolutely, Honoraria," he said, as if in a trance. "I'm terribly sorry".

Eliza threw herself between the vampire and her beloved.

"Don't you touch him," she said fiercely. "And don't do none of them clever mind tricks, neither."

Miss Wellington laughed cruelly and struck Eliza a ferocious blow across the face with the back of her hand. Blood trickled from her lower lip. At the sight, a hideous lustful groan came from Mrs Mordeth, like the Middlesex middle-order man M.W. Gatting presented with a cheese and pickle bloomer.

"Johnny! Think about Yorkshire and the MCC," squealed Eliza.

It seemed to snap him out of his reverie. He grabbed Eliza.

"I've got it! They don't like garlic, do they?" said Johnny. "Or is that French people?"

"No, that's right," said Eliza. "Vampires hate garlic; the French love it. You were thinking of washing."

They looked across the Nursery Ground to the food court.

"How much money have you got?" said Eliza. Johnny began going through his pockets.

"About five guineas, I think."

"Hmm," said Eliza. "Well, it'll have to do. That's what the average man earns in about a year, so we should just be able to afford something from one of the stalls."

They ran to the food court with the bloodthirsty vampire duo snapping at their heels. Pausing to have their tickets checked by stewards just four or five times on the short journey, Eliza eventually managed to purchase a small ham and garlic roll for the price of a modest terraced house in the provinces.

Mrs Mordeth had caught up with them and grabbed at Eliza's shoulder, but Eliza span round and shoved the garlicky snack right in her mouth. Mrs Mordeth burst immediately into flames and combusted entirely before their very eyes.

"Good shot, Eliza," said Johnny.

Miss Wellington let out a chilling scream and flew at Eliza in a rage, but the nimble scullery maid ducked. Eliza and Johnny ran like they had never run before. Soon they made it to the main ground, and Eliza hesitated about setting foot on the hallowed turf.

"It's okay," gasped Johnny. "Perambulation has been permitted during this interval."

They stopped at the square, panting and exhausted in each others' arms.

"What are we going to do, Johnny?" said Eliza. "We cannot run forever."

"Indeed not," said Miss Wellington from behind them, looking as dangerous from the Pavilion End as G.D. McGrath in his pomp.

"I shall so enjoy eating you, child," said Miss Wellington. "How dare you come between me and my pet." She exposed her fangs. Moving staggeringly quickly, she soon had her hands around Eliza's delicate throat.

Johnny yelled and ran to wrestle her off, but Miss Wellington swatted him away as if he were an English medium pacer on a flat track at Sydney. However, Johnny's intervention bought Eliza a fraction of a second. She dived to the wicket at the Nursery End and whipped out a stump. As Miss Wellington pounced, she drove it into the creature's heart. A scream came from Miss Wellington and she exploded all over the turf, roughly on a good length for a spinner. A grotesque stench rose up, and some flames. And then silence, and nothing.

Johnny took Eliza in his arms and kissed her, and together they walked arm-in-arm into the pavilion.

The Long Room rose to applaud them. Eliza was astonished. The President of the MCC strode towards her.

"Well played, young lady," he said. "You certainly dispatched that ghastly vampire woman with some aplomb."

"Sir, yes sir," said Eliza. "But am I to be dismissed from my position? I know I overstepped my boundaries, sir, by killing two women in the afternoon session."

"Not at all, dear girl," said the President benevolently. "You've done us a most valuable service. For many years, females had been clamouring to join the MCC. But now that one of their leading agitators has been revealed to be a vampire, this blessed pavilion will remain unsullied by individuals of the feminine persuasion for ever more."

A great cheer rang out.

"Apart from servants and the occasional harlot, of course," chuckled the President.

The room roared with laughter.

"Actually sir," said Johnny. "If I may make so bold, I would like Eliza to be released from her employment. I wish to take her as my wife."

"I'm afraid that is completely out of the question," said the President. "We could hardly have the captain of MCC marrying a pleb such as yourself, Eliza. No offence."

"Actually, Henry," said a small, elderly voice. "There may be a happy solution."

It was Mr Frindall, the esteemed custodian of the MCC historical records.

"According to my scoresheets, young Eliza was actually born out of wedlock to her mother, a drunken left-handed chambermaid, and the Hon R.O. Shuttleworth of Oxford University and Surrey, who impregnated the woman on a pre-season charity tour of the East End. She may be a bastard, but she's a posh bastard."

"Huzzah!" shouted the room.

Johnny got down on one knee.

"Eliza Shuttleworth, will you do me the honour of being my wife?"

Eliza sighed. She truly was the happiest girl in the world. She gazed down at Johnny.

In horror, she saw his mouth open wide and sharp fangs snap out. He grabbed her. The assorted dignitaries of MCC closed in, hungry for blood. She screamed in terror as the venerable crowd engulfed her, and devoured her in... The Pavilion Of Horrors.

THE END

IN OUR NEXT ISSUE, WE WILL FEATURE A RECENTLY DISCOVERED SERIAL FROM THE PEN OF THE LATE MR ANTHONY TROLLOPE ENTITLED 'CRICKETERS FROM MARS PROPOSITIONED MY WIFE'

ALSO IN THE FORTHCOMING ISSUE!

Should camouflage be allowed on the field of play?... Is the playing of the clarionette a nuisance at Cricket?... The hopes and fears of Mr Steven Finn, including a discussion of male grooming and aggressive pigeons... Ought the Church to rule in the matter of 'reverse swinging'? Engels on Essex... Cricket and the electromagnetic telephone: a warning... Venice: the next cricketing hotbed?... And many other matters of import and entertainment ...

MISS IT AT YOUR PERIL!

LITERATURE

WITH OUR LATE LITERARY
EDITOR 'INKY' PATTERSON

Emboldened by his successful
epistolary intervention in The
Dreyfus Affair, the celebrated
French novelist Emile Zola has
turned his attention to Cricket...

Lettre Au President
De Committee Selective
Anglais (Crickette)
au sujet de L'Affair
Ramprakash

J'ACCUSE!

Je suis absolument fu-
rieux que vous n'avez pas
selecté le batteur magni-
fique de Surrey, Mon-
sieur Mark Rampakash,
pour votre équipe crick-
ette nationale. Depuis
trois ou quatre ans,
Monsieur Ramps n'a pas
de rival dans le Champi-
onship des Countées, et
il a averagé plus de 100.
Une centaine! Quoi plus
doit-il faire?

L'équipe nationale est
plein de batteurs qui ne
sont pas fitte pour enlick-
er les bootes de Ramps,
et je vous presente que
c'est une conspiracee
sinistère parce que
Ramps était sans doubte
un peu d'un nutteur
quand il était plus jeune
('Bloodaxe', etc.).

Si Angleterre est
soixante pour quatre ou
cinq ce hiver contre Les
Aussies, qui préfére-
riez-vous voir en se
promenant au wickette?
Monsieur Ramps, ou ce
petit squitte I.R. Bell?
Ne me fais pas rire.

L'Affair Ramprakash
est une disgrace
nationale et Monsieur
Ramps est le victime de
discrimination parce
qu'il n'est pas 'Un Des
Laddes' qui aime jouer au
jeux de ordinateur, faire
les remarques idiotiques
sur Le Twitteur ou
embracer le cul de le
manageur d'équipe.

Emile Zola (Monsieur)

MRS CECILY BEASTING IS EXTREMELY HONOURED THIS
MONTH TO WELCOME OUR GUEST AGONISING UNCLE, THE
BRILLIANT DR SIGMUND FREUD, WHOSE WRITINGS ON
THE HUMAN MIND ARE AS REVOLUTIONARY AS THEY ARE
ALARMING. DR FREUD, OF COURSE, IS AN EXTREMELY ABLE
CRICKETER WHOSE MEDIUM PACE IS NOTED FOR ITS PROBING
LINE, AND WHOSE LUSTY CONTRIBUTIONS IN THE LOWER-
MIDDLE ORDER HAVE TURNED MANY A GAME BETWEEN
PSYCHOANALYSTS V MANIACS IN HIS NATIVE AUSTRIA.

Dear Dr Freud,

I admire my wife terribly but I am troubled by lurid, not to say feverish, imaginings of her twin brother. I am deeply ashamed of my feelings, and could not bear to hurt or shame my dear wife, but I fear that I will be trapped for ever in this prison of unspoken, unspeakable want.

–H.D. Jessop (Mr)

Dr Freud writes:

This is a clear case of simply playing down the wrong line of a delivery. You must watch the ball closely out of the bowler's hand and focus completely on the movement of your back foot. From your handwriting, I presume you are left-handed, so I am in this instance going to prescribe the taking of a leg-stump guard.

Dear Dr Freud,

Although I am considered a model of respectability amongst my acquaintances, I find myself unconscionably aroused by the thought of women trapped in the lavatory. A serious incident recently took place when I locked the wife of the Member of Parliament for Cheam in the WC at Paddington Station, only narrowly escaping arrest.

—Hon. R. Waldegrave, MP

Dr Freud writes: Here we see a traumatic childhood experience sublimated into sexual feelings in adulthood. Perhaps you were given out timed-out in a school match after a bout of constipation? Or caught short during summer holiday French Cricket and nanny had to take you for a humiliating change of underwear behind the rose garden? Remember in future to pad up in plenty of time, and consider a leg-stump guard.

Dear Dr Freud,

While this may be outside your immediate area of expertise, I have nowhere else to turn. I am currently in the midst of a terrible series of scores for my Cricket team, Gentlemen of Tewksbury, and have made fully six ducks in seven innings. I fancy my stance at the wicket may be askance, or perhaps my back-lift. Have you any advice at all, Dr Freud, for I am quite at my wits' end?

—The Rev. W.T. Cardington

Dr Freud replies: I am in no doubt that your batting difficulties stem from a deeply-rooted and utterly disgusting desire to murder your own father most horribly, before throwing yourself upon your own dear sweet mama and ravaging her as if you were a wild beast. You sicken and repel me, Vicar. Perhaps switch to a leg-stump guard.

NEXT ISSUE: 'IN THE PRIORY'
SUSSEX AND ENGLAND WICKETKEEPER M.J. IRONGLOVE-
PRIOR ADVISES UPON MATTERS OF THE HEART.
DR FREUD WILL NOT BE RETURNING.

PERSONAL NOTICES

A NEW YARN of devilish intrigue involving Sherlock Holmes is to be published later this month, entitled *The Case Of The Missing Number Three*. It finds the unrivalled detective seemingly stumped as to the ongoing selection difficulty afflicting the England Cricket team. Send one shilling to PO Box 221B, London to receive a bound edition.

WILLIAM. I am sorry to inform you of a Third Man. Wilhelmina.

CONFESSIONS Of An English Opium Eater - The Musical! comes to the West End Stage in time for Christmas. It will be performed at Her Majesty's Theatre in Haymarket and is the much-anticipated successor to the acclaimed *Raffles The Gentleman Crackhead* at the same venue. Tickets are available at reduced rates for MCC members or certified drug addicts.

'CRICKET, Masculinity And The Working Man In Yorkshire': a lecture. Assemble Leeds Town Hall, November 5th at six o'clock. Ladies welcome.

CRICKETERS of England. Did the disgraced American industrialist Sir Allen Roosterbender Stanford III Junior attempt to take your wife for an impromptu dicky-back ride around his Cricket Ground or encourage her to participate in a seemingly harmless game of boomps-a-daisy? Contact the Police if you have reason to believe so.

IRISH: you too can join the England cricket team. Apply to Lord's any morning this month, although be sure to leave pigs, etc. tethered neatly outside.

A 24-HOUR PERIOD IN THE DAILY EXISTENCE OF...

E.M. GRACE

THE GLOUCESTERSHIRE BATSMAN, BOWLER, PHYSICIAN AND BROTHER OF W.G. GRACE

SIX O'CLOCK...
Awaken full of excitement, for I have had a most remarkable dream in which I discover a cure for polio. Hurriedly I scribble down some notes and hasten to my laboratory. When I get there, I find my brother William has already cured the disease and is smoking a short pipe with his feet up on my bureau. I am not disheartened.

EIGHT O'CLOCK...
Practise at the pianoforte; I am becoming quite accomplished and can play almost all of *Für Elise.*

A QUARTER PAST EIGHT...
Give up piano, as William has pushed me off it and is performing Beethoven's Ninth on the instrument, while juggling trumpets and reciting Latin witticisms backwards.

ONE O'CLOCK...
I prepare a simple meal of roasted chicken, vegetables and a warming soup.

A QUARTER PAST ONE...
Seeing my menu, William rushes into the kitchen.

THREE O'CLOCK...
I am extremely hungry, but William has insisted that we do not start on luncheon until he is allowed to present his own additional course to the meal. He has made roasted chicken, vegetables and a warming soup. He insists that we throw away the food I have prepared and eat his. Wearily, I acquiesce. In the interests of honesty, I must reluctantly concede that his roasted chicken is slightly tastier than mine.

MIDNIGHT...
William has spent the last nine hours chanting "my chicken was considerably more toothsome than the bird of your own preparation" and bouncing cricket balls off the back of my head as I try to read in the study. I repair to bed.